I0817502

THIS BELONGS TO:

365 DAYS OF GRATITUDE

KEEPING A GRATITUDE JOURNAL is an effective way to feel happier and more motivated in your day-to-day life. Regular attention to this journal will encourage you to focus more on things that inspire and enrich you and less on things that drain your energy and resources.

The prompts in this journal will guide you to reflect on the people, things, and events that fill your heart with appreciation and joy. You can record big accomplishments, like running a marathon, and small delights, like your morning cup of tea. What matters most is that you recognize the good emotions associated with writing gratitude entries and notice how they impact your everyday life.

Designed to be annotated twice a day, this journal prompts you to set out with a positive mood each morning and reflect thankfully on the day's events and emotions each evening. Take your time writing entries, savor every new experience, and enjoy the gifts that gratitude can bring to each moment.

MORNING MEDITATION

DATE __/__/__

TODAY'S FOCUS:

WHAT I'M GRATEFUL FOR:

- ☐
- ☐
- ☐

EVENING REFLECTION

GOOD THINGS THAT HAPPENED TODAY:

HOW FOCUSING ON GRATITUDE MADE ME FEEL:

A POSITIVE THOUGHT TO CARRY ME TO SLEEP:

MORNING MEDITATION

DATE __/__/__

TODAY'S FOCUS:

WHAT I'M GRATEFUL FOR:

- [ ]
- [ ]
- [ ]

EVENING REFLECTION

GOOD THINGS THAT HAPPENED TODAY:

HOW FOCUSING ON GRATITUDE MADE ME FEEL:

A POSITIVE THOUGHT TO CARRY ME TO SLEEP:

MORNING MEDITATION

DATE __/__/__

TODAY'S FOCUS:

WHAT I'M GRATEFUL FOR:

☐

☐

☐

EVENING REFLECTION

GOOD THINGS THAT HAPPENED TODAY:

HOW FOCUSING ON GRATITUDE MADE ME FEEL:

A POSITIVE THOUGHT TO CARRY ME TO SLEEP:

MORNING MEDITATION

DATE __/__/__

TODAY'S FOCUS:

WHAT I'M GRATEFUL FOR:

- [ ]
- [ ]
- [ ]

EVENING REFLECTION

GOOD THINGS THAT HAPPENED TODAY:

HOW FOCUSING ON GRATITUDE MADE ME FEEL:

A POSITIVE THOUGHT TO CARRY ME TO SLEEP:

MORNING MEDITATION

DATE ___/___/___

TODAY'S FOCUS:

WHAT I'M GRATEFUL FOR:

- [ ]
- [ ]
- [ ]

EVENING REFLECTION

GOOD THINGS THAT HAPPENED TODAY:

HOW FOCUSING ON GRATITUDE MADE ME FEEL:

A POSITIVE THOUGHT TO CARRY ME TO SLEEP:

MORNING MEDITATION

DATE ___/___/___

TODAY'S FOCUS:

WHAT I'M GRATEFUL FOR:

- [ ]
- [ ]
- [ ]

EVENING REFLECTION

GOOD THINGS THAT HAPPENED TODAY:

HOW FOCUSING ON GRATITUDE MADE ME FEEL:

A POSITIVE THOUGHT TO CARRY ME TO SLEEP:

MORNING MEDITATION

DATE __/__/__

TODAY'S FOCUS:

WHAT I'M GRATEFUL FOR:

- [ ]
- [ ]
- [ ]

EVENING REFLECTION

GOOD THINGS THAT HAPPENED TODAY:

HOW FOCUSING ON GRATITUDE MADE ME FEEL:

A POSITIVE THOUGHT TO CARRY ME TO SLEEP:

MORNING MEDITATION

DATE ___/___/___

TODAY'S FOCUS:

WHAT I'M GRATEFUL FOR:

- [ ]
- [ ]
- [ ]

EVENING REFLECTION

GOOD THINGS THAT HAPPENED TODAY:

HOW FOCUSING ON GRATITUDE MADE ME FEEL:

A POSITIVE THOUGHT TO CARRY ME TO SLEEP:

MORNING MEDITATION

DATE ___/___/___

TODAY'S FOCUS:

WHAT I'M GRATEFUL FOR:

- [ ]
- [ ]
- [ ]

EVENING REFLECTION

GOOD THINGS THAT HAPPENED TODAY:

HOW FOCUSING ON GRATITUDE MADE ME FEEL:

A POSITIVE THOUGHT TO CARRY ME TO SLEEP:

MORNING MEDITATION

DATE __/__/__

TODAY'S FOCUS:

WHAT I'M GRATEFUL FOR:

☐

☐

☐

EVENING REFLECTION

GOOD THINGS THAT HAPPENED TODAY:

HOW FOCUSING ON GRATITUDE MADE ME FEEL:

A POSITIVE THOUGHT TO CARRY ME TO SLEEP:

MORNING MEDITATION

DATE ___/___/___

TODAY'S FOCUS:

WHAT I'M GRATEFUL FOR:

- [ ]
- [ ]
- [ ]

EVENING REFLECTION

GOOD THINGS THAT HAPPENED TODAY:

HOW FOCUSING ON GRATITUDE MADE ME FEEL:

A POSITIVE THOUGHT TO CARRY ME TO SLEEP:

MORNING MEDITATION

DATE __/__/__

TODAY'S FOCUS:

WHAT I'M GRATEFUL FOR:

- [ ]
- [ ]
- [ ]

EVENING REFLECTION

GOOD THINGS THAT HAPPENED TODAY:

HOW FOCUSING ON GRATITUDE MADE ME FEEL:

A POSITIVE THOUGHT TO CARRY ME TO SLEEP:

MORNING MEDITATION

DATE ___/___/___

TODAY'S FOCUS:

WHAT I'M GRATEFUL FOR:

- [ ]
- [ ]
- [ ]

EVENING REFLECTION

GOOD THINGS THAT HAPPENED TODAY:

HOW FOCUSING ON GRATITUDE MADE ME FEEL:

A POSITIVE THOUGHT TO CARRY ME TO SLEEP:

MORNING MEDITATION

DATE __/__/__

TODAY'S FOCUS:

WHAT I'M GRATEFUL FOR:

- [ ]
- [ ]
- [ ]

EVENING REFLECTION

GOOD THINGS THAT HAPPENED TODAY:

HOW FOCUSING ON GRATITUDE MADE ME FEEL:

A POSITIVE THOUGHT TO CARRY ME TO SLEEP:

MORNING MEDITATION

DATE __/__/__

TODAY'S FOCUS:

WHAT I'M GRATEFUL FOR:

- [ ]
- [ ]
- [ ]

EVENING REFLECTION

GOOD THINGS THAT HAPPENED TODAY:

HOW FOCUSING ON GRATITUDE MADE ME FEEL:

A POSITIVE THOUGHT TO CARRY ME TO SLEEP:

MORNING MEDITATION

DATE __/__/__

TODAY'S FOCUS:

WHAT I'M GRATEFUL FOR:

- [ ]
- [ ]
- [ ]

EVENING REFLECTION

GOOD THINGS THAT HAPPENED TODAY:

HOW FOCUSING ON GRATITUDE MADE ME FEEL:

A POSITIVE THOUGHT TO CARRY ME TO SLEEP:

MORNING MEDITATION

DATE ___/___/___

TODAY'S FOCUS:

WHAT I'M GRATEFUL FOR:

- [ ]
- [ ]
- [ ]

EVENING REFLECTION

GOOD THINGS THAT HAPPENED TODAY:

HOW FOCUSING ON GRATITUDE MADE ME FEEL:

A POSITIVE THOUGHT TO CARRY ME TO SLEEP:

MORNING MEDITATION

DATE ___/___/___

TODAY'S FOCUS:

WHAT I'M GRATEFUL FOR:

- [ ]
- [ ]
- [ ]

EVENING REFLECTION

GOOD THINGS THAT HAPPENED TODAY:

HOW FOCUSING ON GRATITUDE MADE ME FEEL:

A POSITIVE THOUGHT TO CARRY ME TO SLEEP:

MORNING MEDITATION

DATE ___/___/___

TODAY'S FOCUS:

WHAT I'M GRATEFUL FOR:

- [ ]
- [ ]
- [ ]

EVENING REFLECTION

GOOD THINGS THAT HAPPENED TODAY:

HOW FOCUSING ON GRATITUDE MADE ME FEEL:

A POSITIVE THOUGHT TO CARRY ME TO SLEEP:

MORNING MEDITATION

DATE ___/___/___

TODAY'S FOCUS:

WHAT I'M GRATEFUL FOR:

- [ ]
- [ ]
- [ ]

EVENING REFLECTION

GOOD THINGS THAT HAPPENED TODAY:

HOW FOCUSING ON GRATITUDE MADE ME FEEL:

A POSITIVE THOUGHT TO CARRY ME TO SLEEP:

MORNING MEDITATION

DATE __/__/__

TODAY'S FOCUS:

WHAT I'M GRATEFUL FOR:

- [ ]
- [ ]
- [ ]

EVENING REFLECTION

GOOD THINGS THAT HAPPENED TODAY:

HOW FOCUSING ON GRATITUDE MADE ME FEEL:

A POSITIVE THOUGHT TO CARRY ME TO SLEEP:

MORNING MEDITATION

DATE ___/___/___

TODAY'S FOCUS:

WHAT I'M GRATEFUL FOR:

- [ ]
- [ ]
- [ ]

EVENING REFLECTION

GOOD THINGS THAT HAPPENED TODAY:

HOW FOCUSING ON GRATITUDE MADE ME FEEL:

A POSITIVE THOUGHT TO CARRY ME TO SLEEP:

MORNING MEDITATION

DATE ___/___/___

TODAY'S FOCUS:

WHAT I'M GRATEFUL FOR:

- [ ]
- [ ]
- [ ]

EVENING REFLECTION

GOOD THINGS THAT HAPPENED TODAY:

HOW FOCUSING ON GRATITUDE MADE ME FEEL:

A POSITIVE THOUGHT TO CARRY ME TO SLEEP:

MORNING MEDITATION

DATE ___/___/___

TODAY'S FOCUS:

WHAT I'M GRATEFUL FOR:

- [ ]
- [ ]
- [ ]

EVENING REFLECTION

GOOD THINGS THAT HAPPENED TODAY:

HOW FOCUSING ON GRATITUDE MADE ME FEEL:

A POSITIVE THOUGHT TO CARRY ME TO SLEEP:

MORNING MEDITATION

DATE ___/___/___

TODAY'S FOCUS:

WHAT I'M GRATEFUL FOR:

- [ ]
- [ ]
- [ ]

EVENING REFLECTION

GOOD THINGS THAT HAPPENED TODAY:

HOW FOCUSING ON GRATITUDE MADE ME FEEL:

A POSITIVE THOUGHT TO CARRY ME TO SLEEP:

MORNING MEDITATION

DATE __/__/__

TODAY'S FOCUS:

WHAT I'M GRATEFUL FOR:

- [ ]
- [ ]
- [ ]

EVENING REFLECTION

GOOD THINGS THAT HAPPENED TODAY:

HOW FOCUSING ON GRATITUDE MADE ME FEEL:

A POSITIVE THOUGHT TO CARRY ME TO SLEEP:

MORNING MEDITATION

DATE __/__/__

TODAY'S FOCUS:

WHAT I'M GRATEFUL FOR:

- [ ]
- [ ]
- [ ]

EVENING REFLECTION

GOOD THINGS THAT HAPPENED TODAY:

HOW FOCUSING ON GRATITUDE MADE ME FEEL:

A POSITIVE THOUGHT TO CARRY ME TO SLEEP:

MORNING MEDITATION

DATE ___/___/___

TODAY'S FOCUS:

WHAT I'M GRATEFUL FOR:

- [ ]
- [ ]
- [ ]

EVENING REFLECTION

GOOD THINGS THAT HAPPENED TODAY:

HOW FOCUSING ON GRATITUDE MADE ME FEEL:

A POSITIVE THOUGHT TO CARRY ME TO SLEEP:

MORNING MEDITATION

DATE ___/___/

TODAY'S FOCUS:

WHAT I'M GRATEFUL FOR:

- [ ]
- [ ]
- [ ]

EVENING REFLECTION

GOOD THINGS THAT HAPPENED TODAY:

HOW FOCUSING ON GRATITUDE MADE ME FEEL:

A POSITIVE THOUGHT TO CARRY ME TO SLEEP:

MORNING MEDITATION

DATE ___/___/___

TODAY'S FOCUS:

WHAT I'M GRATEFUL FOR:

- [ ]
- [ ]
- [ ]

EVENING REFLECTION

GOOD THINGS THAT HAPPENED TODAY:

HOW FOCUSING ON GRATITUDE MADE ME FEEL:

A POSITIVE THOUGHT TO CARRY ME TO SLEEP:

30-DAY REFLECTION

MONTH:

REFLECTIONS ON THE EFFECTS GRATITUDE HAS HAD ON MY OVERALL WELL BEING AND THE IMPACT IT HAS HAD ON MY EVERYDAY LIFE.

MORNING MEDITATION

DATE __ / __ / __

TODAY'S FOCUS:

WHAT I'M GRATEFUL FOR:

- [ ]
- [ ]
- [ ]

EVENING REFLECTION

GOOD THINGS THAT HAPPENED TODAY:

HOW FOCUSING ON GRATITUDE MADE ME FEEL:

A POSITIVE THOUGHT TO CARRY ME TO SLEEP:

MORNING MEDITATION

DATE __/__/__

TODAY'S FOCUS:

WHAT I'M GRATEFUL FOR:

- [ ]
- [ ]
- [ ]

EVENING REFLECTION

GOOD THINGS THAT HAPPENED TODAY:

HOW FOCUSING ON GRATITUDE MADE ME FEEL:

A POSITIVE THOUGHT TO CARRY ME TO SLEEP:

MORNING MEDITATION

DATE __/__/__

TODAY'S FOCUS:

WHAT I'M GRATEFUL FOR:

☐

☐

☐

EVENING REFLECTION

GOOD THINGS THAT HAPPENED TODAY:

HOW FOCUSING ON GRATITUDE MADE ME FEEL:

A POSITIVE THOUGHT TO CARRY ME TO SLEEP:

MORNING MEDITATION

DATE ___/___/___

TODAY'S FOCUS:

WHAT I'M GRATEFUL FOR:

- [ ]
- [ ]
- [ ]

EVENING REFLECTION

GOOD THINGS THAT HAPPENED TODAY:

HOW FOCUSING ON GRATITUDE MADE ME FEEL:

A POSITIVE THOUGHT TO CARRY ME TO SLEEP:

MORNING MEDITATION

DATE ___/___/___

TODAY'S FOCUS:

WHAT I'M GRATEFUL FOR:

- [ ]
- [ ]
- [ ]

EVENING REFLECTION

GOOD THINGS THAT HAPPENED TODAY:

HOW FOCUSING ON GRATITUDE MADE ME FEEL:

A POSITIVE THOUGHT TO CARRY ME TO SLEEP:

MORNING MEDITATION

DATE ___/___/___

TODAY'S FOCUS:

WHAT I'M GRATEFUL FOR:

- [ ]
- [ ]
- [ ]

EVENING REFLECTION

GOOD THINGS THAT HAPPENED TODAY:

HOW FOCUSING ON GRATITUDE MADE ME FEEL:

A POSITIVE THOUGHT TO CARRY ME TO SLEEP:

MORNING MEDITATION

DATE ___/___/___

TODAY'S FOCUS:

WHAT I'M GRATEFUL FOR:

- [ ]
- [ ]
- [ ]

EVENING REFLECTION

GOOD THINGS THAT HAPPENED TODAY:

HOW FOCUSING ON GRATITUDE MADE ME FEEL:

A POSITIVE THOUGHT TO CARRY ME TO SLEEP:

MORNING MEDITATION

DATE ___/___/___

TODAY'S FOCUS:

WHAT I'M GRATEFUL FOR:

- [ ]
- [ ]
- [ ]

EVENING REFLECTION

GOOD THINGS THAT HAPPENED TODAY:

HOW FOCUSING ON GRATITUDE MADE ME FEEL:

A POSITIVE THOUGHT TO CARRY ME TO SLEEP:

MORNING MEDITATION

DATE ___/___/___

TODAY'S FOCUS:

WHAT I'M GRATEFUL FOR:

☐

☐

☐

EVENING REFLECTION

GOOD THINGS THAT HAPPENED TODAY:

HOW FOCUSING ON GRATITUDE MADE ME FEEL:

A POSITIVE THOUGHT TO CARRY ME TO SLEEP:

MORNING MEDITATION

DATE ___/___/___

TODAY'S FOCUS:

WHAT I'M GRATEFUL FOR:

- [ ]
- [ ]
- [ ]

EVENING REFLECTION

GOOD THINGS THAT HAPPENED TODAY:

HOW FOCUSING ON GRATITUDE MADE ME FEEL:

A POSITIVE THOUGHT TO CARRY ME TO SLEEP:

MORNING MEDITATION

DATE __/__/__

TODAY'S FOCUS:

WHAT I'M GRATEFUL FOR:

- [ ]
- [ ]
- [ ]

EVENING REFLECTION

GOOD THINGS THAT HAPPENED TODAY:

HOW FOCUSING ON GRATITUDE MADE ME FEEL:

A POSITIVE THOUGHT TO CARRY ME TO SLEEP:

MORNING MEDITATION

DATE __/__/__

TODAY'S FOCUS:

WHAT I'M GRATEFUL FOR:

- [ ]
- [ ]
- [ ]

EVENING REFLECTION

GOOD THINGS THAT HAPPENED TODAY:

HOW FOCUSING ON GRATITUDE MADE ME FEEL:

A POSITIVE THOUGHT TO CARRY ME TO SLEEP:

MORNING MEDITATION

DATE __/__/__

TODAY'S FOCUS:

WHAT I'M GRATEFUL FOR:

- ☐
- ☐
- ☐

EVENING REFLECTION

GOOD THINGS THAT HAPPENED TODAY:

HOW FOCUSING ON GRATITUDE MADE ME FEEL:

A POSITIVE THOUGHT TO CARRY ME TO SLEEP:

MORNING MEDITATION

DATE ___/___/___

TODAY'S FOCUS:

WHAT I'M GRATEFUL FOR:

- [ ]
- [ ]
- [ ]

EVENING REFLECTION

GOOD THINGS THAT HAPPENED TODAY:

HOW FOCUSING ON GRATITUDE MADE ME FEEL:

A POSITIVE THOUGHT TO CARRY ME TO SLEEP:

MORNING MEDITATION

DATE ___/___/___

TODAY'S FOCUS:

WHAT I'M GRATEFUL FOR:

- [ ]
- [ ]
- [ ]

EVENING REFLECTION

GOOD THINGS THAT HAPPENED TODAY:

HOW FOCUSING ON GRATITUDE MADE ME FEEL:

A POSITIVE THOUGHT TO CARRY ME TO SLEEP:

MORNING MEDITATION

DATE __/__/__

TODAY'S FOCUS:

WHAT I'M GRATEFUL FOR:

- [ ]
- [ ]
- [ ]

EVENING REFLECTION

GOOD THINGS THAT HAPPENED TODAY:

HOW FOCUSING ON GRATITUDE MADE ME FEEL:

A POSITIVE THOUGHT TO CARRY ME TO SLEEP:

MORNING MEDITATION

DATE __/__/__

TODAY'S FOCUS:

WHAT I'M GRATEFUL FOR:

- [ ]
- [ ]
- [ ]

EVENING REFLECTION

GOOD THINGS THAT HAPPENED TODAY:

HOW FOCUSING ON GRATITUDE MADE ME FEEL:

A POSITIVE THOUGHT TO CARRY ME TO SLEEP:

MORNING MEDITATION

DATE ___/___/___

TODAY'S FOCUS:

WHAT I'M GRATEFUL FOR:

☐

☐

☐

EVENING REFLECTION

GOOD THINGS THAT HAPPENED TODAY:

HOW FOCUSING ON GRATITUDE MADE ME FEEL:

A POSITIVE THOUGHT TO CARRY ME TO SLEEP:

MORNING MEDITATION

DATE ___/___/___

TODAY'S FOCUS:

WHAT I'M GRATEFUL FOR:

- [ ]
- [ ]
- [ ]

EVENING REFLECTION

GOOD THINGS THAT HAPPENED TODAY:

HOW FOCUSING ON GRATITUDE MADE ME FEEL:

A POSITIVE THOUGHT TO CARRY ME TO SLEEP:

MORNING MEDITATION

DATE ___/___/___

TODAY'S FOCUS:

WHAT I'M GRATEFUL FOR:

- [ ]
- [ ]
- [ ]

EVENING REFLECTION

GOOD THINGS THAT HAPPENED TODAY:

HOW FOCUSING ON GRATITUDE MADE ME FEEL:

A POSITIVE THOUGHT TO CARRY ME TO SLEEP:

MORNING MEDITATION

DATE ___/___/___

TODAY'S FOCUS:

WHAT I'M GRATEFUL FOR:

- [ ]
- [ ]
- [ ]

EVENING REFLECTION

GOOD THINGS THAT HAPPENED TODAY:

HOW FOCUSING ON GRATITUDE MADE ME FEEL:

A POSITIVE THOUGHT TO CARRY ME TO SLEEP:

MORNING MEDITATION

DATE ___/___/___

TODAY'S FOCUS:

WHAT I'M GRATEFUL FOR:

- [ ]
- [ ]
- [ ]

EVENING REFLECTION

GOOD THINGS THAT HAPPENED TODAY:

HOW FOCUSING ON GRATITUDE MADE ME FEEL:

A POSITIVE THOUGHT TO CARRY ME TO SLEEP:

MORNING MEDITATION

DATE ___/___/___

TODAY'S FOCUS:

WHAT I'M GRATEFUL FOR:

- [ ]
- [ ]
- [ ]

EVENING REFLECTION

GOOD THINGS THAT HAPPENED TODAY:

HOW FOCUSING ON GRATITUDE MADE ME FEEL:

A POSITIVE THOUGHT TO CARRY ME TO SLEEP:

MORNING MEDITATION

DATE __/__/__

TODAY'S FOCUS:

WHAT I'M GRATEFUL FOR:

- [ ]
- [ ]
- [ ]

EVENING REFLECTION

GOOD THINGS THAT HAPPENED TODAY:

HOW FOCUSING ON GRATITUDE MADE ME FEEL:

A POSITIVE THOUGHT TO CARRY ME TO SLEEP:

MORNING MEDITATION

DATE __/__/__

TODAY'S FOCUS:

WHAT I'M GRATEFUL FOR:

- [ ]
- [ ]
- [ ]

EVENING REFLECTION

GOOD THINGS THAT HAPPENED TODAY:

HOW FOCUSING ON GRATITUDE MADE ME FEEL:

A POSITIVE THOUGHT TO CARRY ME TO SLEEP:

MORNING MEDITATION

DATE __/__/__

TODAY'S FOCUS:

WHAT I'M GRATEFUL FOR:

- [ ]
- [ ]
- [ ]

EVENING REFLECTION

GOOD THINGS THAT HAPPENED TODAY:

HOW FOCUSING ON GRATITUDE MADE ME FEEL:

A POSITIVE THOUGHT TO CARRY ME TO SLEEP:

MORNING MEDITATION

DATE ___/___/___

TODAY'S FOCUS:

WHAT I'M GRATEFUL FOR:

- [ ]
- [ ]
- [ ]

EVENING REFLECTION

GOOD THINGS THAT HAPPENED TODAY:

HOW FOCUSING ON GRATITUDE MADE ME FEEL:

A POSITIVE THOUGHT TO CARRY ME TO SLEEP:

MORNING MEDITATION

DATE ___/___/___

TODAY'S FOCUS:

WHAT I'M GRATEFUL FOR:

- [ ]
- [ ]
- [ ]

EVENING REFLECTION

GOOD THINGS THAT HAPPENED TODAY:

HOW FOCUSING ON GRATITUDE MADE ME FEEL:

A POSITIVE THOUGHT TO CARRY ME TO SLEEP:

MORNING MEDITATION

DATE __/__/__

TODAY'S FOCUS:

WHAT I'M GRATEFUL FOR:

- [ ]
- [ ]
- [ ]

EVENING REFLECTION

GOOD THINGS THAT HAPPENED TODAY:

HOW FOCUSING ON GRATITUDE MADE ME FEEL:

A POSITIVE THOUGHT TO CARRY ME TO SLEEP:

MORNING MEDITATION

DATE ___/___/___

TODAY'S FOCUS:

WHAT I'M GRATEFUL FOR:

- [ ]
- [ ]
- [ ]

EVENING REFLECTION

GOOD THINGS THAT HAPPENED TODAY:

HOW FOCUSING ON GRATITUDE MADE ME FEEL:

A POSITIVE THOUGHT TO CARRY ME TO SLEEP:

30-DAY REFLECTION

MONTH:

REFLECTIONS ON THE EFFECTS GRATITUDE HAS HAD ON MY OVERALL WELL BEING AND THE IMPACT IT HAS HAD ON MY EVERYDAY LIFE.

MORNING MEDITATION

DATE ___/___/___

TODAY'S FOCUS:

WHAT I'M GRATEFUL FOR:

- [ ]
- [ ]
- [ ]

EVENING REFLECTION

GOOD THINGS THAT HAPPENED TODAY:

HOW FOCUSING ON GRATITUDE MADE ME FEEL:

A POSITIVE THOUGHT TO CARRY ME TO SLEEP:

MORNING MEDITATION

DATE ___/___/___

TODAY'S FOCUS:

WHAT I'M GRATEFUL FOR:

- [ ]
- [ ]
- [ ]

EVENING REFLECTION

GOOD THINGS THAT HAPPENED TODAY:

HOW FOCUSING ON GRATITUDE MADE ME FEEL:

A POSITIVE THOUGHT TO CARRY ME TO SLEEP:

MORNING MEDITATION

DATE ___/___/___

TODAY'S FOCUS:

WHAT I'M GRATEFUL FOR:

- [ ]
- [ ]
- [ ]

EVENING REFLECTION

GOOD THINGS THAT HAPPENED TODAY:

HOW FOCUSING ON GRATITUDE MADE ME FEEL:

A POSITIVE THOUGHT TO CARRY ME TO SLEEP:

MORNING MEDITATION

DATE __/__/__

TODAY'S FOCUS:

WHAT I'M GRATEFUL FOR:

- [ ]
- [ ]
- [ ]

EVENING REFLECTION

GOOD THINGS THAT HAPPENED TODAY:

HOW FOCUSING ON GRATITUDE MADE ME FEEL:

A POSITIVE THOUGHT TO CARRY ME TO SLEEP:

MORNING MEDITATION

DATE ___/___/___

TODAY'S FOCUS:

WHAT I'M GRATEFUL FOR:

- [ ]
- [ ]
- [ ]

EVENING REFLECTION

GOOD THINGS THAT HAPPENED TODAY:

HOW FOCUSING ON GRATITUDE MADE ME FEEL:

A POSITIVE THOUGHT TO CARRY ME TO SLEEP:

MORNING MEDITATION

DATE __/__/__

TODAY'S FOCUS:

WHAT I'M GRATEFUL FOR:

- [ ]
- [ ]
- [ ]

EVENING REFLECTION

GOOD THINGS THAT HAPPENED TODAY:

HOW FOCUSING ON GRATITUDE MADE ME FEEL:

A POSITIVE THOUGHT TO CARRY ME TO SLEEP:

MORNING MEDITATION

DATE ___/___/___

TODAY'S FOCUS:

WHAT I'M GRATEFUL FOR:

☐

☐

☐

EVENING REFLECTION

GOOD THINGS THAT HAPPENED TODAY:

HOW FOCUSING ON GRATITUDE MADE ME FEEL:

A POSITIVE THOUGHT TO CARRY ME TO SLEEP:

MORNING MEDITATION

DATE __/__/__

TODAY'S FOCUS:

WHAT I'M GRATEFUL FOR:

- [ ]
- [ ]
- [ ]

EVENING REFLECTION

GOOD THINGS THAT HAPPENED TODAY:

HOW FOCUSING ON GRATITUDE MADE ME FEEL:

A POSITIVE THOUGHT TO CARRY ME TO SLEEP:

MORNING MEDITATION

DATE __/__/__

TODAY'S FOCUS:

WHAT I'M GRATEFUL FOR:

- [ ]
- [ ]
- [ ]

EVENING REFLECTION

GOOD THINGS THAT HAPPENED TODAY:

HOW FOCUSING ON GRATITUDE MADE ME FEEL:

A POSITIVE THOUGHT TO CARRY ME TO SLEEP:

MORNING MEDITATION

DATE ___/___/___

TODAY'S FOCUS:

WHAT I'M GRATEFUL FOR:

- [ ]
- [ ]
- [ ]

EVENING REFLECTION

GOOD THINGS THAT HAPPENED TODAY:

HOW FOCUSING ON GRATITUDE MADE ME FEEL:

A POSITIVE THOUGHT TO CARRY ME TO SLEEP:

MORNING MEDITATION

DATE ___/___/___

TODAY'S FOCUS:

WHAT I'M GRATEFUL FOR:

- [ ]
- [ ]
- [ ]

EVENING REFLECTION

GOOD THINGS THAT HAPPENED TODAY:

HOW FOCUSING ON GRATITUDE MADE ME FEEL:

A POSITIVE THOUGHT TO CARRY ME TO SLEEP:

MORNING MEDITATION

DATE ___/___/___

TODAY'S FOCUS:

WHAT I'M GRATEFUL FOR:

- [ ]
- [ ]
- [ ]

EVENING REFLECTION

GOOD THINGS THAT HAPPENED TODAY:

HOW FOCUSING ON GRATITUDE MADE ME FEEL:

A POSITIVE THOUGHT TO CARRY ME TO SLEEP:

MORNING MEDITATION

DATE ___/___/___

TODAY'S FOCUS:

WHAT I'M GRATEFUL FOR:

- [ ]
- [ ]
- [ ]

EVENING REFLECTION

GOOD THINGS THAT HAPPENED TODAY:

HOW FOCUSING ON GRATITUDE MADE ME FEEL:

A POSITIVE THOUGHT TO CARRY ME TO SLEEP:

MORNING MEDITATION

DATE ___/___/___

TODAY'S FOCUS:

WHAT I'M GRATEFUL FOR:

☐

☐

☐

EVENING REFLECTION

GOOD THINGS THAT HAPPENED TODAY:

HOW FOCUSING ON GRATITUDE MADE ME FEEL:

A POSITIVE THOUGHT TO CARRY ME TO SLEEP:

MORNING MEDITATION

DATE __/__/__

TODAY'S FOCUS:

WHAT I'M GRATEFUL FOR:

- [ ]
- [ ]
- [ ]

EVENING REFLECTION

GOOD THINGS THAT HAPPENED TODAY:

HOW FOCUSING ON GRATITUDE MADE ME FEEL:

A POSITIVE THOUGHT TO CARRY ME TO SLEEP:

MORNING MEDITATION

DATE __/__/__

TODAY'S FOCUS:

WHAT I'M GRATEFUL FOR:

EVENING REFLECTION

GOOD THINGS THAT HAPPENED TODAY:

HOW FOCUSING ON GRATITUDE MADE ME FEEL:

A POSITIVE THOUGHT TO CARRY ME TO SLEEP:

MORNING MEDITATION

DATE __/__/__

TODAY'S FOCUS:

WHAT I'M GRATEFUL FOR:

- [ ]
- [ ]
- [ ]

EVENING REFLECTION

GOOD THINGS THAT HAPPENED TODAY:

HOW FOCUSING ON GRATITUDE MADE ME FEEL:

A POSITIVE THOUGHT TO CARRY ME TO SLEEP:

MORNING MEDITATION

DATE ___/___/___

TODAY'S FOCUS:

WHAT I'M GRATEFUL FOR:

- [ ]
- [ ]
- [ ]

EVENING REFLECTION

GOOD THINGS THAT HAPPENED TODAY:

HOW FOCUSING ON GRATITUDE MADE ME FEEL:

A POSITIVE THOUGHT TO CARRY ME TO SLEEP:

MORNING MEDITATION

DATE __/__/__

TODAY'S FOCUS:

WHAT I'M GRATEFUL FOR:

- [ ]
- [ ]
- [ ]

EVENING REFLECTION

GOOD THINGS THAT HAPPENED TODAY:

HOW FOCUSING ON GRATITUDE MADE ME FEEL:

A POSITIVE THOUGHT TO CARRY ME TO SLEEP:

MORNING MEDITATION

DATE ___/___/___

TODAY'S FOCUS:

WHAT I'M GRATEFUL FOR:

- [ ]
- [ ]
- [ ]

EVENING REFLECTION

GOOD THINGS THAT HAPPENED TODAY:

HOW FOCUSING ON GRATITUDE MADE ME FEEL:

A POSITIVE THOUGHT TO CARRY ME TO SLEEP:

MORNING MEDITATION

DATE __/__/__

TODAY'S FOCUS:

WHAT I'M GRATEFUL FOR:

- [ ]
- [ ]
- [ ]

EVENING REFLECTION

GOOD THINGS THAT HAPPENED TODAY:

HOW FOCUSING ON GRATITUDE MADE ME FEEL:

A POSITIVE THOUGHT TO CARRY ME TO SLEEP:

MORNING MEDITATION

DATE ___/___/___

TODAY'S FOCUS:

WHAT I'M GRATEFUL FOR:

EVENING REFLECTION

GOOD THINGS THAT HAPPENED TODAY:

HOW FOCUSING ON GRATITUDE MADE ME FEEL:

A POSITIVE THOUGHT TO CARRY ME TO SLEEP:

MORNING MEDITATION

DATE __/__/__

TODAY'S FOCUS:

WHAT I'M GRATEFUL FOR:

- [ ]
- [ ]
- [ ]

EVENING REFLECTION

GOOD THINGS THAT HAPPENED TODAY:

HOW FOCUSING ON GRATITUDE MADE ME FEEL:

A POSITIVE THOUGHT TO CARRY ME TO SLEEP:

MORNING MEDITATION

DATE __/__/__

TODAY'S FOCUS:

WHAT I'M GRATEFUL FOR:

☐

☐

☐

EVENING REFLECTION

GOOD THINGS THAT HAPPENED TODAY:

HOW FOCUSING ON GRATITUDE MADE ME FEEL:

A POSITIVE THOUGHT TO CARRY ME TO SLEEP:

MORNING MEDITATION

DATE ___/___/___

TODAY'S FOCUS:

WHAT I'M GRATEFUL FOR:

- [ ]
- [ ]
- [ ]

EVENING REFLECTION

GOOD THINGS THAT HAPPENED TODAY:

HOW FOCUSING ON GRATITUDE MADE ME FEEL:

A POSITIVE THOUGHT TO CARRY ME TO SLEEP:

MORNING MEDITATION

DATE ___/___/___

TODAY'S FOCUS:

WHAT I'M GRATEFUL FOR:

- [ ]
- [ ]
- [ ]

EVENING REFLECTION

GOOD THINGS THAT HAPPENED TODAY:

HOW FOCUSING ON GRATITUDE MADE ME FEEL:

A POSITIVE THOUGHT TO CARRY ME TO SLEEP:

MORNING MEDITATION

DATE ___/___/___

TODAY'S FOCUS:

WHAT I'M GRATEFUL FOR:

- ☐
- ☐
- ☐

EVENING REFLECTION

GOOD THINGS THAT HAPPENED TODAY:

HOW FOCUSING ON GRATITUDE MADE ME FEEL:

A POSITIVE THOUGHT TO CARRY ME TO SLEEP:

MORNING MEDITATION

DATE __/__/__

TODAY'S FOCUS:

WHAT I'M GRATEFUL FOR:

☐

☐

☐

EVENING REFLECTION

GOOD THINGS THAT HAPPENED TODAY:

HOW FOCUSING ON GRATITUDE MADE ME FEEL:

A POSITIVE THOUGHT TO CARRY ME TO SLEEP:

MORNING MEDITATION

DATE __/__/__

TODAY'S FOCUS:

WHAT I'M GRATEFUL FOR:

- [ ]
- [ ]
- [ ]

EVENING REFLECTION

GOOD THINGS THAT HAPPENED TODAY:

HOW FOCUSING ON GRATITUDE MADE ME FEEL:

A POSITIVE THOUGHT TO CARRY ME TO SLEEP:

MORNING MEDITATION

DATE __/__/__

TODAY'S FOCUS:

WHAT I'M GRATEFUL FOR:

☐

☐

☐

EVENING REFLECTION

GOOD THINGS THAT HAPPENED TODAY:

HOW FOCUSING ON GRATITUDE MADE ME FEEL:

A POSITIVE THOUGHT TO CARRY ME TO SLEEP:

30-DAY REFLECTION

MONTH:

REFLECTIONS ON THE EFFECTS GRATITUDE HAS HAD ON MY OVERALL WELL BEING AND THE IMPACT IT HAS HAD ON MY EVERYDAY LIFE.

MORNING MEDITATION

DATE ___/___/___

TODAY'S FOCUS:

WHAT I'M GRATEFUL FOR:

- [ ]
- [ ]
- [ ]

EVENING REFLECTION

GOOD THINGS THAT HAPPENED TODAY:

HOW FOCUSING ON GRATITUDE MADE ME FEEL:

A POSITIVE THOUGHT TO CARRY ME TO SLEEP:

MORNING MEDITATION

DATE ___/___/___

TODAY'S FOCUS:

WHAT I'M GRATEFUL FOR:

- [ ]
- [ ]
- [ ]

EVENING REFLECTION

GOOD THINGS THAT HAPPENED TODAY:

HOW FOCUSING ON GRATITUDE MADE ME FEEL:

A POSITIVE THOUGHT TO CARRY ME TO SLEEP:

MORNING MEDITATION

DATE __/__/__

TODAY'S FOCUS:

WHAT I'M GRATEFUL FOR:

- [ ]
- [ ]
- [ ]

EVENING REFLECTION

GOOD THINGS THAT HAPPENED TODAY:

HOW FOCUSING ON GRATITUDE MADE ME FEEL:

A POSITIVE THOUGHT TO CARRY ME TO SLEEP:

MORNING MEDITATION

DATE ___/___/___

TODAY'S FOCUS:

WHAT I'M GRATEFUL FOR:

- [ ]
- [ ]
- [ ]

EVENING REFLECTION

GOOD THINGS THAT HAPPENED TODAY:

HOW FOCUSING ON GRATITUDE MADE ME FEEL:

A POSITIVE THOUGHT TO CARRY ME TO SLEEP:

MORNING MEDITATION

DATE __/__/__

TODAY'S FOCUS:

WHAT I'M GRATEFUL FOR:

- [ ]
- [ ]
- [ ]

EVENING REFLECTION

GOOD THINGS THAT HAPPENED TODAY:

HOW FOCUSING ON GRATITUDE MADE ME FEEL:

A POSITIVE THOUGHT TO CARRY ME TO SLEEP:

MORNING MEDITATION

DATE ___/___/___

TODAY'S FOCUS:

WHAT I'M GRATEFUL FOR:

- [ ]
- [ ]
- [ ]

EVENING REFLECTION

GOOD THINGS THAT HAPPENED TODAY:

HOW FOCUSING ON GRATITUDE MADE ME FEEL:

A POSITIVE THOUGHT TO CARRY ME TO SLEEP:

MORNING MEDITATION

DATE ___/___/___

TODAY'S FOCUS:

WHAT I'M GRATEFUL FOR:

- [ ]
- [ ]
- [ ]

EVENING REFLECTION

GOOD THINGS THAT HAPPENED TODAY:

HOW FOCUSING ON GRATITUDE MADE ME FEEL:

A POSITIVE THOUGHT TO CARRY ME TO SLEEP:

MORNING MEDITATION

DATE ___/___/___

TODAY'S FOCUS:

WHAT I'M GRATEFUL FOR:

- [ ]
- [ ]
- [ ]

EVENING REFLECTION

GOOD THINGS THAT HAPPENED TODAY:

HOW FOCUSING ON GRATITUDE MADE ME FEEL:

A POSITIVE THOUGHT TO CARRY ME TO SLEEP:

MORNING MEDITATION

DATE ___/___/___

TODAY'S FOCUS:

WHAT I'M GRATEFUL FOR:

- [ ]
- [ ]
- [ ]

EVENING REFLECTION

GOOD THINGS THAT HAPPENED TODAY:

HOW FOCUSING ON GRATITUDE MADE ME FEEL:

A POSITIVE THOUGHT TO CARRY ME TO SLEEP:

MORNING MEDITATION

DATE __/__/__

TODAY'S FOCUS:

WHAT I'M GRATEFUL FOR:

- [ ]
- [ ]
- [ ]

EVENING REFLECTION

GOOD THINGS THAT HAPPENED TODAY:

HOW FOCUSING ON GRATITUDE MADE ME FEEL:

A POSITIVE THOUGHT TO CARRY ME TO SLEEP:

MORNING MEDITATION

DATE ___/___/___

TODAY'S FOCUS:

WHAT I'M GRATEFUL FOR:

- [ ]
- [ ]
- [ ]

EVENING REFLECTION

GOOD THINGS THAT HAPPENED TODAY:

HOW FOCUSING ON GRATITUDE MADE ME FEEL:

A POSITIVE THOUGHT TO CARRY ME TO SLEEP:

MORNING MEDITATION

DATE ___/___/___

TODAY'S FOCUS:

WHAT I'M GRATEFUL FOR:

- [ ]
- [ ]
- [ ]

EVENING REFLECTION

GOOD THINGS THAT HAPPENED TODAY:

HOW FOCUSING ON GRATITUDE MADE ME FEEL:

A POSITIVE THOUGHT TO CARRY ME TO SLEEP:

MORNING MEDITATION

DATE ___/___/___

TODAY'S FOCUS:

WHAT I'M GRATEFUL FOR:

- [ ]
- [ ]
- [ ]

EVENING REFLECTION

GOOD THINGS THAT HAPPENED TODAY:

HOW FOCUSING ON GRATITUDE MADE ME FEEL:

A POSITIVE THOUGHT TO CARRY ME TO SLEEP:

MORNING MEDITATION

DATE __/__/__

TODAY'S FOCUS:

WHAT I'M GRATEFUL FOR:

☐

☐

☐

EVENING REFLECTION

GOOD THINGS THAT HAPPENED TODAY:

HOW FOCUSING ON GRATITUDE MADE ME FEEL:

A POSITIVE THOUGHT TO CARRY ME TO SLEEP:

MORNING MEDITATION

DATE __/__/__

TODAY'S FOCUS:

WHAT I'M GRATEFUL FOR:

- [ ]
- [ ]
- [ ]

EVENING REFLECTION

GOOD THINGS THAT HAPPENED TODAY:

HOW FOCUSING ON GRATITUDE MADE ME FEEL:

A POSITIVE THOUGHT TO CARRY ME TO SLEEP:

MORNING MEDITATION

DATE __/__/__

TODAY'S FOCUS:

WHAT I'M GRATEFUL FOR:

- [ ]
- [ ]
- [ ]

EVENING REFLECTION

GOOD THINGS THAT HAPPENED TODAY:

HOW FOCUSING ON GRATITUDE MADE ME FEEL:

A POSITIVE THOUGHT TO CARRY ME TO SLEEP:

MORNING MEDITATION

DATE ___/___/___

TODAY'S FOCUS:

WHAT I'M GRATEFUL FOR:

- [ ]
- [ ]
- [ ]

EVENING REFLECTION

GOOD THINGS THAT HAPPENED TODAY:

HOW FOCUSING ON GRATITUDE MADE ME FEEL:

A POSITIVE THOUGHT TO CARRY ME TO SLEEP:

MORNING MEDITATION

DATE __/__/__

TODAY'S FOCUS:

WHAT I'M GRATEFUL FOR:

- [ ]
- [ ]
- [ ]

EVENING REFLECTION

GOOD THINGS THAT HAPPENED TODAY:

HOW FOCUSING ON GRATITUDE MADE ME FEEL:

A POSITIVE THOUGHT TO CARRY ME TO SLEEP:

MORNING MEDITATION

DATE __/__/__

TODAY'S FOCUS:

WHAT I'M GRATEFUL FOR:

☐

☐

☐

EVENING REFLECTION

GOOD THINGS THAT HAPPENED TODAY:

HOW FOCUSING ON GRATITUDE MADE ME FEEL:

A POSITIVE THOUGHT TO CARRY ME TO SLEEP:

MORNING MEDITATION

DATE __/__/__

TODAY'S FOCUS:

WHAT I'M GRATEFUL FOR:

- [ ]
- [ ]
- [ ]

EVENING REFLECTION

GOOD THINGS THAT HAPPENED TODAY:

HOW FOCUSING ON GRATITUDE MADE ME FEEL:

A POSITIVE THOUGHT TO CARRY ME TO SLEEP:

MORNING MEDITATION

DATE ___/___/___

TODAY'S FOCUS:

WHAT I'M GRATEFUL FOR:

- [ ]
- [ ]
- [ ]

EVENING REFLECTION

GOOD THINGS THAT HAPPENED TODAY:

HOW FOCUSING ON GRATITUDE MADE ME FEEL:

A POSITIVE THOUGHT TO CARRY ME TO SLEEP:

MORNING MEDITATION

DATE ___/___/___

TODAY'S FOCUS:

WHAT I'M GRATEFUL FOR:

- [ ]
- [ ]
- [ ]

EVENING REFLECTION

GOOD THINGS THAT HAPPENED TODAY:

HOW FOCUSING ON GRATITUDE MADE ME FEEL:

A POSITIVE THOUGHT TO CARRY ME TO SLEEP:

MORNING MEDITATION

DATE ___/___/___

TODAY'S FOCUS:

WHAT I'M GRATEFUL FOR:

- ☐
- ☐
- ☐

EVENING REFLECTION

GOOD THINGS THAT HAPPENED TODAY:

HOW FOCUSING ON GRATITUDE MADE ME FEEL:

A POSITIVE THOUGHT TO CARRY ME TO SLEEP:

MORNING MEDITATION

DATE ___/___/___

TODAY'S FOCUS:

WHAT I'M GRATEFUL FOR:

- [ ]
- [ ]
- [ ]

EVENING REFLECTION

GOOD THINGS THAT HAPPENED TODAY:

HOW FOCUSING ON GRATITUDE MADE ME FEEL:

A POSITIVE THOUGHT TO CARRY ME TO SLEEP:

MORNING MEDITATION

DATE __/__/__

TODAY'S FOCUS:

WHAT I'M GRATEFUL FOR:

- [ ]
- [ ]
- [ ]

EVENING REFLECTION

GOOD THINGS THAT HAPPENED TODAY:

HOW FOCUSING ON GRATITUDE MADE ME FEEL:

A POSITIVE THOUGHT TO CARRY ME TO SLEEP:

MORNING MEDITATION

DATE ___/___/___

TODAY'S FOCUS:

WHAT I'M GRATEFUL FOR:

- [ ]
- [ ]
- [ ]

EVENING REFLECTION

GOOD THINGS THAT HAPPENED TODAY:

HOW FOCUSING ON GRATITUDE MADE ME FEEL:

A POSITIVE THOUGHT TO CARRY ME TO SLEEP:

MORNING MEDITATION

DATE ___/___/___

TODAY'S FOCUS:

WHAT I'M GRATEFUL FOR:

- [ ]
- [ ]
- [ ]

EVENING REFLECTION

GOOD THINGS THAT HAPPENED TODAY:

HOW FOCUSING ON GRATITUDE MADE ME FEEL:

A POSITIVE THOUGHT TO CARRY ME TO SLEEP:

MORNING MEDITATION

DATE ___/___/___

TODAY'S FOCUS:

WHAT I'M GRATEFUL FOR:

- [ ]
- [ ]
- [ ]

EVENING REFLECTION

GOOD THINGS THAT HAPPENED TODAY:

HOW FOCUSING ON GRATITUDE MADE ME FEEL:

A POSITIVE THOUGHT TO CARRY ME TO SLEEP:

MORNING MEDITATION

DATE __/__/__

TODAY'S FOCUS:

WHAT I'M GRATEFUL FOR:

☐

☐

☐

EVENING REFLECTION

GOOD THINGS THAT HAPPENED TODAY:

HOW FOCUSING ON GRATITUDE MADE ME FEEL:

A POSITIVE THOUGHT TO CARRY ME TO SLEEP:

MORNING MEDITATION

DATE ___/___/___

TODAY'S FOCUS:

WHAT I'M GRATEFUL FOR:

- [ ]
- [ ]
- [ ]

EVENING REFLECTION

GOOD THINGS THAT HAPPENED TODAY:

HOW FOCUSING ON GRATITUDE MADE ME FEEL:

A POSITIVE THOUGHT TO CARRY ME TO SLEEP:

30-DAY REFLECTION

MONTH:

REFLECTIONS ON THE EFFECTS GRATITUDE HAS HAD ON MY OVERALL WELL BEING AND THE IMPACT IT HAS HAD ON MY EVERYDAY LIFE.

MORNING MEDITATION

DATE ___/___/___

TODAY'S FOCUS:

WHAT I'M GRATEFUL FOR:

- [ ]
- [ ]
- [ ]

EVENING REFLECTION

GOOD THINGS THAT HAPPENED TODAY:

HOW FOCUSING ON GRATITUDE MADE ME FEEL:

A POSITIVE THOUGHT TO CARRY ME TO SLEEP:

MORNING MEDITATION

DATE __/__/__

TODAY'S FOCUS:

WHAT I'M GRATEFUL FOR:

- [ ]
- [ ]
- [ ]

EVENING REFLECTION

GOOD THINGS THAT HAPPENED TODAY:

HOW FOCUSING ON GRATITUDE MADE ME FEEL:

A POSITIVE THOUGHT TO CARRY ME TO SLEEP:

MORNING MEDITATION

DATE __/__/__

TODAY'S FOCUS:

WHAT I'M GRATEFUL FOR:

- [ ]
- [ ]
- [ ]

EVENING REFLECTION

GOOD THINGS THAT HAPPENED TODAY:

HOW FOCUSING ON GRATITUDE MADE ME FEEL:

A POSITIVE THOUGHT TO CARRY ME TO SLEEP:

MORNING MEDITATION

DATE __/__/__

TODAY'S FOCUS:

WHAT I'M GRATEFUL FOR:

- [ ]
- [ ]
- [ ]

EVENING REFLECTION

GOOD THINGS THAT HAPPENED TODAY:

HOW FOCUSING ON GRATITUDE MADE ME FEEL:

A POSITIVE THOUGHT TO CARRY ME TO SLEEP:

MORNING MEDITATION

DATE ___/___/___

TODAY'S FOCUS:

WHAT I'M GRATEFUL FOR:

- [ ]
- [ ]
- [ ]

EVENING REFLECTION

GOOD THINGS THAT HAPPENED TODAY:

HOW FOCUSING ON GRATITUDE MADE ME FEEL:

A POSITIVE THOUGHT TO CARRY ME TO SLEEP:

MORNING MEDITATION

DATE __/__/__

TODAY'S FOCUS:

WHAT I'M GRATEFUL FOR:

- [ ]
- [ ]
- [ ]

EVENING REFLECTION

GOOD THINGS THAT HAPPENED TODAY:

HOW FOCUSING ON GRATITUDE MADE ME FEEL:

A POSITIVE THOUGHT TO CARRY ME TO SLEEP:

MORNING MEDITATION

DATE __/__/__

TODAY'S FOCUS:

WHAT I'M GRATEFUL FOR:

- [ ]
- [ ]
- [ ]

EVENING REFLECTION

GOOD THINGS THAT HAPPENED TODAY:

HOW FOCUSING ON GRATITUDE MADE ME FEEL:

A POSITIVE THOUGHT TO CARRY ME TO SLEEP:

MORNING MEDITATION

DATE ___/___/___

TODAY'S FOCUS:

WHAT I'M GRATEFUL FOR:

- [ ]
- [ ]
- [ ]

EVENING REFLECTION

GOOD THINGS THAT HAPPENED TODAY:

HOW FOCUSING ON GRATITUDE MADE ME FEEL:

A POSITIVE THOUGHT TO CARRY ME TO SLEEP:

MORNING MEDITATION

DATE ___/___/___

TODAY'S FOCUS:

WHAT I'M GRATEFUL FOR:

- [ ]
- [ ]
- [ ]

EVENING REFLECTION

GOOD THINGS THAT HAPPENED TODAY:

HOW FOCUSING ON GRATITUDE MADE ME FEEL:

A POSITIVE THOUGHT TO CARRY ME TO SLEEP:

MORNING MEDITATION

DATE ___/___/___

TODAY'S FOCUS:

WHAT I'M GRATEFUL FOR:

- [ ]
- [ ]
- [ ]

EVENING REFLECTION

GOOD THINGS THAT HAPPENED TODAY:

HOW FOCUSING ON GRATITUDE MADE ME FEEL:

A POSITIVE THOUGHT TO CARRY ME TO SLEEP:

MORNING MEDITATION

DATE ___/___/___

TODAY'S FOCUS:

WHAT I'M GRATEFUL FOR:

- ☐
- ☐
- ☐

EVENING REFLECTION

GOOD THINGS THAT HAPPENED TODAY:

HOW FOCUSING ON GRATITUDE MADE ME FEEL:

A POSITIVE THOUGHT TO CARRY ME TO SLEEP:

MORNING MEDITATION

DATE ___/___/___

TODAY'S FOCUS:

WHAT I'M GRATEFUL FOR:

☐

☐

☐

EVENING REFLECTION

GOOD THINGS THAT HAPPENED TODAY:

HOW FOCUSING ON GRATITUDE MADE ME FEEL:

A POSITIVE THOUGHT TO CARRY ME TO SLEEP:

MORNING MEDITATION

DATE ___/___/___

TODAY'S FOCUS:

WHAT I'M GRATEFUL FOR:

- [ ]
- [ ]
- [ ]

EVENING REFLECTION

GOOD THINGS THAT HAPPENED TODAY:

HOW FOCUSING ON GRATITUDE MADE ME FEEL:

A POSITIVE THOUGHT TO CARRY ME TO SLEEP:

MORNING MEDITATION

DATE __/__/__

TODAY'S FOCUS:

WHAT I'M GRATEFUL FOR:

- [ ]
- [ ]
- [ ]

EVENING REFLECTION

GOOD THINGS THAT HAPPENED TODAY:

HOW FOCUSING ON GRATITUDE MADE ME FEEL:

A POSITIVE THOUGHT TO CARRY ME TO SLEEP:

MORNING MEDITATION

DATE ___/___/___

TODAY'S FOCUS:

WHAT I'M GRATEFUL FOR:

- [ ]
- [ ]
- [ ]

EVENING REFLECTION

GOOD THINGS THAT HAPPENED TODAY:

HOW FOCUSING ON GRATITUDE MADE ME FEEL:

A POSITIVE THOUGHT TO CARRY ME TO SLEEP:

MORNING MEDITATION

DATE __/__/__

TODAY'S FOCUS:

WHAT I'M GRATEFUL FOR:

- [ ]
- [ ]
- [ ]

EVENING REFLECTION

GOOD THINGS THAT HAPPENED TODAY:

HOW FOCUSING ON GRATITUDE MADE ME FEEL:

A POSITIVE THOUGHT TO CARRY ME TO SLEEP:

MORNING MEDITATION

DATE ___/___/___

TODAY'S FOCUS:

WHAT I'M GRATEFUL FOR:

- [ ]
- [ ]
- [ ]

EVENING REFLECTION

GOOD THINGS THAT HAPPENED TODAY:

HOW FOCUSING ON GRATITUDE MADE ME FEEL:

A POSITIVE THOUGHT TO CARRY ME TO SLEEP:

MORNING MEDITATION

DATE ___/___/___

TODAY'S FOCUS:

WHAT I'M GRATEFUL FOR:

- [ ]
- [ ]
- [ ]

EVENING REFLECTION

GOOD THINGS THAT HAPPENED TODAY:

HOW FOCUSING ON GRATITUDE MADE ME FEEL:

A POSITIVE THOUGHT TO CARRY ME TO SLEEP:

MORNING MEDITATION

DATE ___/___/___

TODAY'S FOCUS:

WHAT I'M GRATEFUL FOR:

- [ ]
- [ ]
- [ ]

EVENING REFLECTION

GOOD THINGS THAT HAPPENED TODAY:

HOW FOCUSING ON GRATITUDE MADE ME FEEL:

A POSITIVE THOUGHT TO CARRY ME TO SLEEP:

MORNING MEDITATION

DATE ___/___/___

TODAY'S FOCUS:

WHAT I'M GRATEFUL FOR:

- [ ]
- [ ]
- [ ]

EVENING REFLECTION

GOOD THINGS THAT HAPPENED TODAY:

HOW FOCUSING ON GRATITUDE MADE ME FEEL:

A POSITIVE THOUGHT TO CARRY ME TO SLEEP:

MORNING MEDITATION

DATE ___/___/___

TODAY'S FOCUS:

WHAT I'M GRATEFUL FOR:

- [ ]
- [ ]
- [ ]

EVENING REFLECTION

GOOD THINGS THAT HAPPENED TODAY:

HOW FOCUSING ON GRATITUDE MADE ME FEEL:

A POSITIVE THOUGHT TO CARRY ME TO SLEEP:

MORNING MEDITATION

DATE ___/___/___

TODAY'S FOCUS:

WHAT I'M GRATEFUL FOR:

EVENING REFLECTION

GOOD THINGS THAT HAPPENED TODAY:

HOW FOCUSING ON GRATITUDE MADE ME FEEL:

A POSITIVE THOUGHT TO CARRY ME TO SLEEP:

MORNING MEDITATION

DATE __/__/__

TODAY'S FOCUS:

WHAT I'M GRATEFUL FOR:

- ☐
- ☐
- ☐

EVENING REFLECTION

GOOD THINGS THAT HAPPENED TODAY:

HOW FOCUSING ON GRATITUDE MADE ME FEEL:

A POSITIVE THOUGHT TO CARRY ME TO SLEEP:

MORNING MEDITATION

DATE ___/___/___

TODAY'S FOCUS:

WHAT I'M GRATEFUL FOR:

- [ ]
- [ ]
- [ ]

EVENING REFLECTION

GOOD THINGS THAT HAPPENED TODAY:

HOW FOCUSING ON GRATITUDE MADE ME FEEL:

A POSITIVE THOUGHT TO CARRY ME TO SLEEP:

MORNING MEDITATION

DATE __/__/__

TODAY'S FOCUS:

WHAT I'M GRATEFUL FOR:

- [ ]
- [ ]
- [ ]

EVENING REFLECTION

GOOD THINGS THAT HAPPENED TODAY:

HOW FOCUSING ON GRATITUDE MADE ME FEEL:

A POSITIVE THOUGHT TO CARRY ME TO SLEEP:

MORNING MEDITATION

DATE ___/___/___

TODAY'S FOCUS:

WHAT I'M GRATEFUL FOR:

- ☐
- ☐
- ☐

EVENING REFLECTION

GOOD THINGS THAT HAPPENED TODAY:

HOW FOCUSING ON GRATITUDE MADE ME FEEL:

A POSITIVE THOUGHT TO CARRY ME TO SLEEP:

MORNING MEDITATION

DATE ___/___/___

TODAY'S FOCUS:

WHAT I'M GRATEFUL FOR:

- [ ]
- [ ]
- [ ]

EVENING REFLECTION

GOOD THINGS THAT HAPPENED TODAY:

HOW FOCUSING ON GRATITUDE MADE ME FEEL:

A POSITIVE THOUGHT TO CARRY ME TO SLEEP:

MORNING MEDITATION

DATE ___/___/___

TODAY'S FOCUS:

WHAT I'M GRATEFUL FOR:

- [ ]
- [ ]
- [ ]

EVENING REFLECTION

GOOD THINGS THAT HAPPENED TODAY:

HOW FOCUSING ON GRATITUDE MADE ME FEEL:

A POSITIVE THOUGHT TO CARRY ME TO SLEEP:

MORNING MEDITATION

DATE ___/___/___

TODAY'S FOCUS:

WHAT I'M GRATEFUL FOR:

- [ ]
- [ ]
- [ ]

EVENING REFLECTION

GOOD THINGS THAT HAPPENED TODAY:

HOW FOCUSING ON GRATITUDE MADE ME FEEL:

A POSITIVE THOUGHT TO CARRY ME TO SLEEP:

MORNING MEDITATION

DATE ___/___/___

TODAY'S FOCUS:

WHAT I'M GRATEFUL FOR:

- [ ]
- [ ]
- [ ]

EVENING REFLECTION

GOOD THINGS THAT HAPPENED TODAY:

HOW FOCUSING ON GRATITUDE MADE ME FEEL:

A POSITIVE THOUGHT TO CARRY ME TO SLEEP:

30-DAY REFLECTION

MONTH:

REFLECTIONS ON THE EFFECTS GRATITUDE HAS HAD ON MY OVERALL WELL BEING AND THE IMPACT IT HAS HAD ON MY EVERYDAY LIFE.

MORNING MEDITATION

DATE ___/___/___

TODAY'S FOCUS:

WHAT I'M GRATEFUL FOR:

- [ ]
- [ ]
- [ ]

EVENING REFLECTION

GOOD THINGS THAT HAPPENED TODAY:

HOW FOCUSING ON GRATITUDE MADE ME FEEL:

A POSITIVE THOUGHT TO CARRY ME TO SLEEP:

MORNING MEDITATION

DATE ___/___/___

TODAY'S FOCUS:

WHAT I'M GRATEFUL FOR:

- [ ]
- [ ]
- [ ]

EVENING REFLECTION

GOOD THINGS THAT HAPPENED TODAY:

HOW FOCUSING ON GRATITUDE MADE ME FEEL:

A POSITIVE THOUGHT TO CARRY ME TO SLEEP:

MORNING MEDITATION

DATE ___/___/___

TODAY'S FOCUS:

WHAT I'M GRATEFUL FOR:

- [ ]
- [ ]
- [ ]

EVENING REFLECTION

GOOD THINGS THAT HAPPENED TODAY:

HOW FOCUSING ON GRATITUDE MADE ME FEEL:

A POSITIVE THOUGHT TO CARRY ME TO SLEEP:

MORNING MEDITATION

DATE ___/___/___

TODAY'S FOCUS:

WHAT I'M GRATEFUL FOR:

- [ ]
- [ ]
- [ ]

EVENING REFLECTION

GOOD THINGS THAT HAPPENED TODAY:

HOW FOCUSING ON GRATITUDE MADE ME FEEL:

A POSITIVE THOUGHT TO CARRY ME TO SLEEP:

MORNING MEDITATION

DATE ___/___/___

TODAY'S FOCUS:

WHAT I'M GRATEFUL FOR:

- [ ]
- [ ]
- [ ]

EVENING REFLECTION

GOOD THINGS THAT HAPPENED TODAY:

HOW FOCUSING ON GRATITUDE MADE ME FEEL:

A POSITIVE THOUGHT TO CARRY ME TO SLEEP:

MORNING MEDITATION

DATE ___/___/___

TODAY'S FOCUS:

WHAT I'M GRATEFUL FOR:

- [ ]
- [ ]
- [ ]

EVENING REFLECTION

GOOD THINGS THAT HAPPENED TODAY:

HOW FOCUSING ON GRATITUDE MADE ME FEEL:

A POSITIVE THOUGHT TO CARRY ME TO SLEEP:

MORNING MEDITATION

DATE ___/___/___

TODAY'S FOCUS:

WHAT I'M GRATEFUL FOR:

- [ ]
- [ ]
- [ ]

EVENING REFLECTION

GOOD THINGS THAT HAPPENED TODAY:

HOW FOCUSING ON GRATITUDE MADE ME FEEL:

A POSITIVE THOUGHT TO CARRY ME TO SLEEP:

MORNING MEDITATION

DATE __/__/__

TODAY'S FOCUS:

WHAT I'M GRATEFUL FOR:

- [ ]
- [ ]
- [ ]

EVENING REFLECTION

GOOD THINGS THAT HAPPENED TODAY:

HOW FOCUSING ON GRATITUDE MADE ME FEEL:

A POSITIVE THOUGHT TO CARRY ME TO SLEEP:

MORNING MEDITATION

DATE ___/___/___

TODAY'S FOCUS:

WHAT I'M GRATEFUL FOR:

- [ ]
- [ ]
- [ ]

EVENING REFLECTION

GOOD THINGS THAT HAPPENED TODAY:

HOW FOCUSING ON GRATITUDE MADE ME FEEL:

A POSITIVE THOUGHT TO CARRY ME TO SLEEP:

MORNING MEDITATION

DATE ___/___/___

TODAY'S FOCUS:

WHAT I'M GRATEFUL FOR:

- [ ]
- [ ]
- [ ]

EVENING REFLECTION

GOOD THINGS THAT HAPPENED TODAY:

HOW FOCUSING ON GRATITUDE MADE ME FEEL:

A POSITIVE THOUGHT TO CARRY ME TO SLEEP:

MORNING MEDITATION

DATE __/__/__

TODAY'S FOCUS:

WHAT I'M GRATEFUL FOR:

☐

☐

☐

EVENING REFLECTION

GOOD THINGS THAT HAPPENED TODAY:

HOW FOCUSING ON GRATITUDE MADE ME FEEL:

A POSITIVE THOUGHT TO CARRY ME TO SLEEP:

MORNING MEDITATION

DATE __/__/__

TODAY'S FOCUS:

WHAT I'M GRATEFUL FOR:

- [ ]
- [ ]
- [ ]

EVENING REFLECTION

GOOD THINGS THAT HAPPENED TODAY:

HOW FOCUSING ON GRATITUDE MADE ME FEEL:

A POSITIVE THOUGHT TO CARRY ME TO SLEEP:

MORNING MEDITATION

DATE ___/___/___

TODAY'S FOCUS:

WHAT I'M GRATEFUL FOR:

- [ ]
- [ ]
- [ ]

EVENING REFLECTION

GOOD THINGS THAT HAPPENED TODAY:

HOW FOCUSING ON GRATITUDE MADE ME FEEL:

A POSITIVE THOUGHT TO CARRY ME TO SLEEP:

MORNING MEDITATION

DATE __/__/__

TODAY'S FOCUS:

WHAT I'M GRATEFUL FOR:

- [ ]
- [ ]
- [ ]

EVENING REFLECTION

GOOD THINGS THAT HAPPENED TODAY:

HOW FOCUSING ON GRATITUDE MADE ME FEEL:

A POSITIVE THOUGHT TO CARRY ME TO SLEEP:

MORNING MEDITATION

DATE __/__/__

TODAY'S FOCUS:

WHAT I'M GRATEFUL FOR:

- [ ]
- [ ]
- [ ]

EVENING REFLECTION

GOOD THINGS THAT HAPPENED TODAY:

HOW FOCUSING ON GRATITUDE MADE ME FEEL:

A POSITIVE THOUGHT TO CARRY ME TO SLEEP:

MORNING MEDITATION

DATE ___/___/___

TODAY'S FOCUS:

WHAT I'M GRATEFUL FOR:

- [ ]
- [ ]
- [ ]

EVENING REFLECTION

GOOD THINGS THAT HAPPENED TODAY:

HOW FOCUSING ON GRATITUDE MADE ME FEEL:

A POSITIVE THOUGHT TO CARRY ME TO SLEEP:

MORNING MEDITATION

DATE ___/___/___

TODAY'S FOCUS:

WHAT I'M GRATEFUL FOR:

- [ ]
- [ ]
- [ ]

EVENING REFLECTION

GOOD THINGS THAT HAPPENED TODAY:

HOW FOCUSING ON GRATITUDE MADE ME FEEL:

A POSITIVE THOUGHT TO CARRY ME TO SLEEP:

MORNING MEDITATION

DATE __/__/__

TODAY'S FOCUS:

WHAT I'M GRATEFUL FOR:

- [ ]
- [ ]
- [ ]

EVENING REFLECTION

GOOD THINGS THAT HAPPENED TODAY:

HOW FOCUSING ON GRATITUDE MADE ME FEEL:

A POSITIVE THOUGHT TO CARRY ME TO SLEEP:

MORNING MEDITATION

DATE __/__/__

TODAY'S FOCUS:

WHAT I'M GRATEFUL FOR:

- [ ]
- [ ]
- [ ]

EVENING REFLECTION

GOOD THINGS THAT HAPPENED TODAY:

HOW FOCUSING ON GRATITUDE MADE ME FEEL:

A POSITIVE THOUGHT TO CARRY ME TO SLEEP:

MORNING MEDITATION

DATE ___/___/___

TODAY'S FOCUS:

WHAT I'M GRATEFUL FOR:

- [ ]
- [ ]
- [ ]

EVENING REFLECTION

GOOD THINGS THAT HAPPENED TODAY:

HOW FOCUSING ON GRATITUDE MADE ME FEEL:

A POSITIVE THOUGHT TO CARRY ME TO SLEEP:

MORNING MEDITATION

DATE ___/___/___

TODAY'S FOCUS:

WHAT I'M GRATEFUL FOR:

- [ ]
- [ ]
- [ ]

EVENING REFLECTION

GOOD THINGS THAT HAPPENED TODAY:

HOW FOCUSING ON GRATITUDE MADE ME FEEL:

A POSITIVE THOUGHT TO CARRY ME TO SLEEP:

MORNING MEDITATION

DATE ___/___/___

TODAY'S FOCUS:

WHAT I'M GRATEFUL FOR:

- [ ]
- [ ]
- [ ]

EVENING REFLECTION

GOOD THINGS THAT HAPPENED TODAY:

HOW FOCUSING ON GRATITUDE MADE ME FEEL:

A POSITIVE THOUGHT TO CARRY ME TO SLEEP:

MORNING MEDITATION

DATE __/__/__

TODAY'S FOCUS:

WHAT I'M GRATEFUL FOR:

- [ ]
- [ ]
- [ ]

EVENING REFLECTION

GOOD THINGS THAT HAPPENED TODAY:

HOW FOCUSING ON GRATITUDE MADE ME FEEL:

A POSITIVE THOUGHT TO CARRY ME TO SLEEP:

MORNING MEDITATION

DATE __/__/__

TODAY'S FOCUS:

WHAT I'M GRATEFUL FOR:

- [ ]
- [ ]
- [ ]

EVENING REFLECTION

GOOD THINGS THAT HAPPENED TODAY:

HOW FOCUSING ON GRATITUDE MADE ME FEEL:

A POSITIVE THOUGHT TO CARRY ME TO SLEEP:

MORNING MEDITATION

DATE ___/___/___

TODAY'S FOCUS:

WHAT I'M GRATEFUL FOR:

- [ ]
- [ ]
- [ ]

EVENING REFLECTION

GOOD THINGS THAT HAPPENED TODAY:

HOW FOCUSING ON GRATITUDE MADE ME FEEL:

A POSITIVE THOUGHT TO CARRY ME TO SLEEP:

MORNING MEDITATION

DATE __/__/__

TODAY'S FOCUS:

WHAT I'M GRATEFUL FOR:

- [ ]
- [ ]
- [ ]

EVENING REFLECTION

GOOD THINGS THAT HAPPENED TODAY:

HOW FOCUSING ON GRATITUDE MADE ME FEEL:

A POSITIVE THOUGHT TO CARRY ME TO SLEEP:

MORNING MEDITATION

DATE ___/___/___

TODAY'S FOCUS:

WHAT I'M GRATEFUL FOR:

☐

☐

☐

EVENING REFLECTION

GOOD THINGS THAT HAPPENED TODAY:

HOW FOCUSING ON GRATITUDE MADE ME FEEL:

A POSITIVE THOUGHT TO CARRY ME TO SLEEP:

MORNING MEDITATION

DATE __/__/__

TODAY'S FOCUS:

WHAT I'M GRATEFUL FOR:

- [ ]
- [ ]
- [ ]

EVENING REFLECTION

GOOD THINGS THAT HAPPENED TODAY:

HOW FOCUSING ON GRATITUDE MADE ME FEEL:

A POSITIVE THOUGHT TO CARRY ME TO SLEEP:

MORNING MEDITATION

DATE ___/___/___

TODAY'S FOCUS:

WHAT I'M GRATEFUL FOR:

- [ ]
- [ ]
- [ ]

EVENING REFLECTION

GOOD THINGS THAT HAPPENED TODAY:

HOW FOCUSING ON GRATITUDE MADE ME FEEL:

A POSITIVE THOUGHT TO CARRY ME TO SLEEP:

MORNING MEDITATION

DATE ___/___/___

TODAY'S FOCUS:

WHAT I'M GRATEFUL FOR:

- [ ]
- [ ]
- [ ]

EVENING REFLECTION

GOOD THINGS THAT HAPPENED TODAY:

HOW FOCUSING ON GRATITUDE MADE ME FEEL:

A POSITIVE THOUGHT TO CARRY ME TO SLEEP:

30-DAY REFLECTION

MONTH:

REFLECTIONS ON THE EFFECTS GRATITUDE HAS HAD ON MY OVERALL WELL BEING AND THE IMPACT IT HAS HAD ON MY EVERYDAY LIFE.

MORNING MEDITATION

DATE __/__/__

TODAY'S FOCUS:

WHAT I'M GRATEFUL FOR:

- [ ]
- [ ]
- [ ]

EVENING REFLECTION

GOOD THINGS THAT HAPPENED TODAY:

HOW FOCUSING ON GRATITUDE MADE ME FEEL:

A POSITIVE THOUGHT TO CARRY ME TO SLEEP:

MORNING MEDITATION

DATE ___/___/___

TODAY'S FOCUS:

WHAT I'M GRATEFUL FOR:

- [ ]
- [ ]
- [ ]

EVENING REFLECTION

GOOD THINGS THAT HAPPENED TODAY:

HOW FOCUSING ON GRATITUDE MADE ME FEEL:

A POSITIVE THOUGHT TO CARRY ME TO SLEEP:

MORNING MEDITATION

DATE ___/___/___

TODAY'S FOCUS:

WHAT I'M GRATEFUL FOR:

EVENING REFLECTION

GOOD THINGS THAT HAPPENED TODAY:

HOW FOCUSING ON GRATITUDE MADE ME FEEL:

A POSITIVE THOUGHT TO CARRY ME TO SLEEP:

MORNING MEDITATION

DATE __/__/__

TODAY'S FOCUS:

WHAT I'M GRATEFUL FOR:

- [ ]
- [ ]
- [ ]

EVENING REFLECTION

GOOD THINGS THAT HAPPENED TODAY:

HOW FOCUSING ON GRATITUDE MADE ME FEEL:

A POSITIVE THOUGHT TO CARRY ME TO SLEEP:

MORNING MEDITATION

DATE ___/___/___

TODAY'S FOCUS:

WHAT I'M GRATEFUL FOR:

- [ ]
- [ ]
- [ ]

EVENING REFLECTION

GOOD THINGS THAT HAPPENED TODAY:

HOW FOCUSING ON GRATITUDE MADE ME FEEL:

A POSITIVE THOUGHT TO CARRY ME TO SLEEP:

MORNING MEDITATION

DATE __/__/__

TODAY'S FOCUS:

WHAT I'M GRATEFUL FOR:

- [ ]
- [ ]
- [ ]

EVENING REFLECTION

GOOD THINGS THAT HAPPENED TODAY:

HOW FOCUSING ON GRATITUDE MADE ME FEEL:

A POSITIVE THOUGHT TO CARRY ME TO SLEEP:

MORNING MEDITATION

DATE ___/___/___

TODAY'S FOCUS:

WHAT I'M GRATEFUL FOR:

- [ ]
- [ ]
- [ ]

EVENING REFLECTION

GOOD THINGS THAT HAPPENED TODAY:

HOW FOCUSING ON GRATITUDE MADE ME FEEL:

A POSITIVE THOUGHT TO CARRY ME TO SLEEP:

MORNING MEDITATION

DATE __/__/__

TODAY'S FOCUS:

WHAT I'M GRATEFUL FOR:

- [ ]
- [ ]
- [ ]

EVENING REFLECTION

GOOD THINGS THAT HAPPENED TODAY:

HOW FOCUSING ON GRATITUDE MADE ME FEEL:

A POSITIVE THOUGHT TO CARRY ME TO SLEEP:

MORNING MEDITATION

DATE ___/___/___

TODAY'S FOCUS:

WHAT I'M GRATEFUL FOR:

- [ ]
- [ ]
- [ ]

EVENING REFLECTION

GOOD THINGS THAT HAPPENED TODAY:

HOW FOCUSING ON GRATITUDE MADE ME FEEL:

A POSITIVE THOUGHT TO CARRY ME TO SLEEP:

MORNING MEDITATION

DATE __/__/__

TODAY'S FOCUS:

WHAT I'M GRATEFUL FOR:

- [ ]
- [ ]
- [ ]

EVENING REFLECTION

GOOD THINGS THAT HAPPENED TODAY:

HOW FOCUSING ON GRATITUDE MADE ME FEEL:

A POSITIVE THOUGHT TO CARRY ME TO SLEEP:

MORNING MEDITATION

DATE ___/___/___

TODAY'S FOCUS:

WHAT I'M GRATEFUL FOR:

☐

☐

☐

EVENING REFLECTION

GOOD THINGS THAT HAPPENED TODAY:

HOW FOCUSING ON GRATITUDE MADE ME FEEL:

A POSITIVE THOUGHT TO CARRY ME TO SLEEP:

MORNING MEDITATION

DATE __/__/__

TODAY'S FOCUS:

WHAT I'M GRATEFUL FOR:

- [ ]
- [ ]
- [ ]

EVENING REFLECTION

GOOD THINGS THAT HAPPENED TODAY:

HOW FOCUSING ON GRATITUDE MADE ME FEEL:

A POSITIVE THOUGHT TO CARRY ME TO SLEEP:

MORNING MEDITATION

DATE __/__/__

TODAY'S FOCUS:

WHAT I'M GRATEFUL FOR:

- [ ]
- [ ]
- [ ]

EVENING REFLECTION

GOOD THINGS THAT HAPPENED TODAY:

HOW FOCUSING ON GRATITUDE MADE ME FEEL:

A POSITIVE THOUGHT TO CARRY ME TO SLEEP:

MORNING MEDITATION

DATE __/__/__

TODAY'S FOCUS:

WHAT I'M GRATEFUL FOR:

- [ ]
- [ ]
- [ ]

EVENING REFLECTION

GOOD THINGS THAT HAPPENED TODAY:

HOW FOCUSING ON GRATITUDE MADE ME FEEL:

A POSITIVE THOUGHT TO CARRY ME TO SLEEP:

MORNING MEDITATION

DATE ___/___/___

TODAY'S FOCUS:

WHAT I'M GRATEFUL FOR:

- [ ]
- [ ]
- [ ]

EVENING REFLECTION

GOOD THINGS THAT HAPPENED TODAY:

HOW FOCUSING ON GRATITUDE MADE ME FEEL:

A POSITIVE THOUGHT TO CARRY ME TO SLEEP:

MORNING MEDITATION

DATE __/__/__

TODAY'S FOCUS:

WHAT I'M GRATEFUL FOR:

- [ ]
- [ ]
- [ ]

EVENING REFLECTION

GOOD THINGS THAT HAPPENED TODAY:

HOW FOCUSING ON GRATITUDE MADE ME FEEL:

A POSITIVE THOUGHT TO CARRY ME TO SLEEP:

MORNING MEDITATION

DATE ___/___/___

TODAY'S FOCUS:

WHAT I'M GRATEFUL FOR:

- [ ]
- [ ]
- [ ]

EVENING REFLECTION

GOOD THINGS THAT HAPPENED TODAY:

HOW FOCUSING ON GRATITUDE MADE ME FEEL:

A POSITIVE THOUGHT TO CARRY ME TO SLEEP:

MORNING MEDITATION

DATE __/__/__

TODAY'S FOCUS:

WHAT I'M GRATEFUL FOR:

- [ ]
- [ ]
- [ ]

EVENING REFLECTION

GOOD THINGS THAT HAPPENED TODAY:

HOW FOCUSING ON GRATITUDE MADE ME FEEL:

A POSITIVE THOUGHT TO CARRY ME TO SLEEP:

MORNING MEDITATION

DATE __/__/__

TODAY'S FOCUS:

WHAT I'M GRATEFUL FOR:

- [ ]
- [ ]
- [ ]

EVENING REFLECTION

GOOD THINGS THAT HAPPENED TODAY:

HOW FOCUSING ON GRATITUDE MADE ME FEEL:

A POSITIVE THOUGHT TO CARRY ME TO SLEEP:

MORNING MEDITATION

DATE __/__/__

TODAY'S FOCUS:

WHAT I'M GRATEFUL FOR:

- [ ]
- [ ]
- [ ]

EVENING REFLECTION

GOOD THINGS THAT HAPPENED TODAY:

HOW FOCUSING ON GRATITUDE MADE ME FEEL:

A POSITIVE THOUGHT TO CARRY ME TO SLEEP:

MORNING MEDITATION

DATE __/__/__

TODAY'S FOCUS:

WHAT I'M GRATEFUL FOR:

☐

☐

☐

EVENING REFLECTION

GOOD THINGS THAT HAPPENED TODAY:

HOW FOCUSING ON GRATITUDE MADE ME FEEL:

A POSITIVE THOUGHT TO CARRY ME TO SLEEP:

MORNING MEDITATION

DATE __/__/__

TODAY'S FOCUS:

WHAT I'M GRATEFUL FOR:

- [ ]
- [ ]
- [ ]

EVENING REFLECTION

GOOD THINGS THAT HAPPENED TODAY:

HOW FOCUSING ON GRATITUDE MADE ME FEEL:

A POSITIVE THOUGHT TO CARRY ME TO SLEEP:

MORNING MEDITATION

DATE ___/___/___

TODAY'S FOCUS:

WHAT I'M GRATEFUL FOR:

- [ ]
- [ ]
- [ ]

EVENING REFLECTION

GOOD THINGS THAT HAPPENED TODAY:

HOW FOCUSING ON GRATITUDE MADE ME FEEL:

A POSITIVE THOUGHT TO CARRY ME TO SLEEP:

MORNING MEDITATION

DATE ___/___/___

TODAY'S FOCUS:

WHAT I'M GRATEFUL FOR:

- [ ]
- [ ]
- [ ]

EVENING REFLECTION

GOOD THINGS THAT HAPPENED TODAY:

HOW FOCUSING ON GRATITUDE MADE ME FEEL:

A POSITIVE THOUGHT TO CARRY ME TO SLEEP:

MORNING MEDITATION

DATE __/__/__

TODAY'S FOCUS:

WHAT I'M GRATEFUL FOR:

- [ ]
- [ ]
- [ ]

EVENING REFLECTION

GOOD THINGS THAT HAPPENED TODAY:

HOW FOCUSING ON GRATITUDE MADE ME FEEL:

A POSITIVE THOUGHT TO CARRY ME TO SLEEP:

MORNING MEDITATION

DATE ___/___/___

TODAY'S FOCUS:

WHAT I'M GRATEFUL FOR:

- [ ]
- [ ]
- [ ]

EVENING REFLECTION

GOOD THINGS THAT HAPPENED TODAY:

HOW FOCUSING ON GRATITUDE MADE ME FEEL:

A POSITIVE THOUGHT TO CARRY ME TO SLEEP:

MORNING MEDITATION

DATE __/__/__

TODAY'S FOCUS:

WHAT I'M GRATEFUL FOR:

- [ ]
- [ ]
- [ ]

EVENING REFLECTION

GOOD THINGS THAT HAPPENED TODAY:

HOW FOCUSING ON GRATITUDE MADE ME FEEL:

A POSITIVE THOUGHT TO CARRY ME TO SLEEP:

MORNING MEDITATION

DATE __/__/__

TODAY'S FOCUS:

WHAT I'M GRATEFUL FOR:

- [ ]
- [ ]
- [ ]

EVENING REFLECTION

GOOD THINGS THAT HAPPENED TODAY:

HOW FOCUSING ON GRATITUDE MADE ME FEEL:

A POSITIVE THOUGHT TO CARRY ME TO SLEEP:

MORNING MEDITATION

DATE ___/___/___

TODAY'S FOCUS:

WHAT I'M GRATEFUL FOR:

- [ ]
- [ ]
- [ ]

EVENING REFLECTION

GOOD THINGS THAT HAPPENED TODAY:

HOW FOCUSING ON GRATITUDE MADE ME FEEL:

A POSITIVE THOUGHT TO CARRY ME TO SLEEP:

MORNING MEDITATION

DATE __/__/__

TODAY'S FOCUS:

WHAT I'M GRATEFUL FOR:

☐

☐

☐

EVENING REFLECTION

GOOD THINGS THAT HAPPENED TODAY:

HOW FOCUSING ON GRATITUDE MADE ME FEEL:

A POSITIVE THOUGHT TO CARRY ME TO SLEEP:

30-DAY REFLECTION

MONTH:

REFLECTIONS ON THE EFFECTS GRATITUDE HAS HAD ON MY OVERALL WELL BEING AND THE IMPACT IT HAS HAD ON MY EVERYDAY LIFE.

MORNING MEDITATION

DATE ___/___/___

TODAY'S FOCUS:

WHAT I'M GRATEFUL FOR:

- ☐
- ☐
- ☐

EVENING REFLECTION

GOOD THINGS THAT HAPPENED TODAY:

HOW FOCUSING ON GRATITUDE MADE ME FEEL:

A POSITIVE THOUGHT TO CARRY ME TO SLEEP:

MORNING MEDITATION

DATE ___/___/___

TODAY'S FOCUS:

WHAT I'M GRATEFUL FOR:

- [ ]
- [ ]
- [ ]

EVENING REFLECTION

GOOD THINGS THAT HAPPENED TODAY:

HOW FOCUSING ON GRATITUDE MADE ME FEEL:

A POSITIVE THOUGHT TO CARRY ME TO SLEEP:

MORNING MEDITATION

DATE ___/___/___

TODAY'S FOCUS:

WHAT I'M GRATEFUL FOR:

- [ ]
- [ ]
- [ ]

EVENING REFLECTION

GOOD THINGS THAT HAPPENED TODAY:

HOW FOCUSING ON GRATITUDE MADE ME FEEL:

A POSITIVE THOUGHT TO CARRY ME TO SLEEP:

MORNING MEDITATION

DATE ___/___/___

TODAY'S FOCUS:

WHAT I'M GRATEFUL FOR:

- [ ]
- [ ]
- [ ]

EVENING REFLECTION

GOOD THINGS THAT HAPPENED TODAY:

HOW FOCUSING ON GRATITUDE MADE ME FEEL:

A POSITIVE THOUGHT TO CARRY ME TO SLEEP:

MORNING MEDITATION

DATE __/__/__

TODAY'S FOCUS:

WHAT I'M GRATEFUL FOR:

- [ ]
- [ ]
- [ ]

EVENING REFLECTION

GOOD THINGS THAT HAPPENED TODAY:

HOW FOCUSING ON GRATITUDE MADE ME FEEL:

A POSITIVE THOUGHT TO CARRY ME TO SLEEP:

MORNING MEDITATION

DATE __/__/__

TODAY'S FOCUS:

WHAT I'M GRATEFUL FOR:

☐

☐

☐

EVENING REFLECTION

GOOD THINGS THAT HAPPENED TODAY:

HOW FOCUSING ON GRATITUDE MADE ME FEEL:

A POSITIVE THOUGHT TO CARRY ME TO SLEEP:

MORNING MEDITATION

DATE ___/___/___

TODAY'S FOCUS:

WHAT I'M GRATEFUL FOR:

- [ ]
- [ ]
- [ ]

EVENING REFLECTION

GOOD THINGS THAT HAPPENED TODAY:

HOW FOCUSING ON GRATITUDE MADE ME FEEL:

A POSITIVE THOUGHT TO CARRY ME TO SLEEP:

MORNING MEDITATION

DATE __/__/__

TODAY'S FOCUS:

WHAT I'M GRATEFUL FOR:

- ☐
- ☐
- ☐

EVENING REFLECTION

GOOD THINGS THAT HAPPENED TODAY:

HOW FOCUSING ON GRATITUDE MADE ME FEEL:

A POSITIVE THOUGHT TO CARRY ME TO SLEEP:

MORNING MEDITATION

DATE ___/___/___

TODAY'S FOCUS:

WHAT I'M GRATEFUL FOR:

- [ ]
- [ ]
- [ ]

EVENING REFLECTION

GOOD THINGS THAT HAPPENED TODAY:

HOW FOCUSING ON GRATITUDE MADE ME FEEL:

A POSITIVE THOUGHT TO CARRY ME TO SLEEP:

MORNING MEDITATION

DATE __/__/__

TODAY'S FOCUS:

WHAT I'M GRATEFUL FOR:

- [ ]
- [ ]
- [ ]

EVENING REFLECTION

GOOD THINGS THAT HAPPENED TODAY:

HOW FOCUSING ON GRATITUDE MADE ME FEEL:

A POSITIVE THOUGHT TO CARRY ME TO SLEEP:

MORNING MEDITATION

DATE ___/___/___

TODAY'S FOCUS:

WHAT I'M GRATEFUL FOR:

- [ ]
- [ ]
- [ ]

EVENING REFLECTION

GOOD THINGS THAT HAPPENED TODAY:

HOW FOCUSING ON GRATITUDE MADE ME FEEL:

A POSITIVE THOUGHT TO CARRY ME TO SLEEP:

MORNING MEDITATION

DATE __/__/__

TODAY'S FOCUS:

WHAT I'M GRATEFUL FOR:

- [ ]
- [ ]
- [ ]

EVENING REFLECTION

GOOD THINGS THAT HAPPENED TODAY:

HOW FOCUSING ON GRATITUDE MADE ME FEEL:

A POSITIVE THOUGHT TO CARRY ME TO SLEEP:

MORNING MEDITATION

DATE ___/___/___

TODAY'S FOCUS:

WHAT I'M GRATEFUL FOR:

- [ ]
- [ ]
- [ ]

EVENING REFLECTION

GOOD THINGS THAT HAPPENED TODAY:

HOW FOCUSING ON GRATITUDE MADE ME FEEL:

A POSITIVE THOUGHT TO CARRY ME TO SLEEP:

MORNING MEDITATION

DATE __/__/__

TODAY'S FOCUS:

WHAT I'M GRATEFUL FOR:

- [ ]
- [ ]
- [ ]

EVENING REFLECTION

GOOD THINGS THAT HAPPENED TODAY:

HOW FOCUSING ON GRATITUDE MADE ME FEEL:

A POSITIVE THOUGHT TO CARRY ME TO SLEEP:

MORNING MEDITATION

DATE ___/___/___

TODAY'S FOCUS:

WHAT I'M GRATEFUL FOR:

- [ ]
- [ ]
- [ ]

EVENING REFLECTION

GOOD THINGS THAT HAPPENED TODAY:

HOW FOCUSING ON GRATITUDE MADE ME FEEL:

A POSITIVE THOUGHT TO CARRY ME TO SLEEP:

MORNING MEDITATION

DATE __/__/__

TODAY'S FOCUS:

WHAT I'M GRATEFUL FOR:

- [ ]
- [ ]
- [ ]

EVENING REFLECTION

GOOD THINGS THAT HAPPENED TODAY:

HOW FOCUSING ON GRATITUDE MADE ME FEEL:

A POSITIVE THOUGHT TO CARRY ME TO SLEEP:

MORNING MEDITATION

DATE ___/___/___

TODAY'S FOCUS:

WHAT I'M GRATEFUL FOR:

- [ ]
- [ ]
- [ ]

EVENING REFLECTION

GOOD THINGS THAT HAPPENED TODAY:

HOW FOCUSING ON GRATITUDE MADE ME FEEL:

A POSITIVE THOUGHT TO CARRY ME TO SLEEP:

MORNING MEDITATION

DATE ___/___/___

TODAY'S FOCUS:

WHAT I'M GRATEFUL FOR:

- [ ]
- [ ]
- [ ]

EVENING REFLECTION

GOOD THINGS THAT HAPPENED TODAY:

HOW FOCUSING ON GRATITUDE MADE ME FEEL:

A POSITIVE THOUGHT TO CARRY ME TO SLEEP:

MORNING MEDITATION

DATE ___/___/___

TODAY'S FOCUS:

WHAT I'M GRATEFUL FOR:

- [ ]
- [ ]
- [ ]

EVENING REFLECTION

GOOD THINGS THAT HAPPENED TODAY:

HOW FOCUSING ON GRATITUDE MADE ME FEEL:

A POSITIVE THOUGHT TO CARRY ME TO SLEEP:

MORNING MEDITATION

DATE ___/___/___

TODAY'S FOCUS:

WHAT I'M GRATEFUL FOR:

- [ ]
- [ ]
- [ ]

EVENING REFLECTION

GOOD THINGS THAT HAPPENED TODAY:

HOW FOCUSING ON GRATITUDE MADE ME FEEL:

A POSITIVE THOUGHT TO CARRY ME TO SLEEP:

MORNING MEDITATION

DATE __/__/__

TODAY'S FOCUS:

WHAT I'M GRATEFUL FOR:

- [ ]
- [ ]
- [ ]

EVENING REFLECTION

GOOD THINGS THAT HAPPENED TODAY:

HOW FOCUSING ON GRATITUDE MADE ME FEEL:

A POSITIVE THOUGHT TO CARRY ME TO SLEEP:

MORNING MEDITATION

DATE ___/___/___

TODAY'S FOCUS:

WHAT I'M GRATEFUL FOR:

- [ ]
- [ ]
- [ ]

EVENING REFLECTION

GOOD THINGS THAT HAPPENED TODAY:

HOW FOCUSING ON GRATITUDE MADE ME FEEL:

A POSITIVE THOUGHT TO CARRY ME TO SLEEP:

MORNING MEDITATION

DATE ___/___/___

TODAY'S FOCUS:

WHAT I'M GRATEFUL FOR:

- [ ]
- [ ]
- [ ]

EVENING REFLECTION

GOOD THINGS THAT HAPPENED TODAY:

HOW FOCUSING ON GRATITUDE MADE ME FEEL:

A POSITIVE THOUGHT TO CARRY ME TO SLEEP:

MORNING MEDITATION

DATE ___/___/___

TODAY'S FOCUS:

WHAT I'M GRATEFUL FOR:

- [ ]
- [ ]
- [ ]

EVENING REFLECTION

GOOD THINGS THAT HAPPENED TODAY:

HOW FOCUSING ON GRATITUDE MADE ME FEEL:

A POSITIVE THOUGHT TO CARRY ME TO SLEEP:

MORNING MEDITATION

DATE ___/___/___

TODAY'S FOCUS:

WHAT I'M GRATEFUL FOR:

- [ ]
- [ ]
- [ ]

EVENING REFLECTION

GOOD THINGS THAT HAPPENED TODAY:

HOW FOCUSING ON GRATITUDE MADE ME FEEL:

A POSITIVE THOUGHT TO CARRY ME TO SLEEP:

MORNING MEDITATION

DATE ___/___/___

TODAY'S FOCUS:

WHAT I'M GRATEFUL FOR:

- [ ]
- [ ]
- [ ]

EVENING REFLECTION

GOOD THINGS THAT HAPPENED TODAY:

HOW FOCUSING ON GRATITUDE MADE ME FEEL:

A POSITIVE THOUGHT TO CARRY ME TO SLEEP:

MORNING MEDITATION

DATE __/__/__

TODAY'S FOCUS:

WHAT I'M GRATEFUL FOR:

EVENING REFLECTION

GOOD THINGS THAT HAPPENED TODAY:

HOW FOCUSING ON GRATITUDE MADE ME FEEL:

A POSITIVE THOUGHT TO CARRY ME TO SLEEP:

MORNING MEDITATION

DATE __/__/__

TODAY'S FOCUS:

WHAT I'M GRATEFUL FOR:

- [ ]
- [ ]
- [ ]

EVENING REFLECTION

GOOD THINGS THAT HAPPENED TODAY:

HOW FOCUSING ON GRATITUDE MADE ME FEEL:

A POSITIVE THOUGHT TO CARRY ME TO SLEEP:

MORNING MEDITATION

DATE __/__/__

TODAY'S FOCUS:

WHAT I'M GRATEFUL FOR:

- ☐
- ☐
- ☐

EVENING REFLECTION

GOOD THINGS THAT HAPPENED TODAY:

HOW FOCUSING ON GRATITUDE MADE ME FEEL:

A POSITIVE THOUGHT TO CARRY ME TO SLEEP:

MORNING MEDITATION

DATE __/__/__

TODAY'S FOCUS:

WHAT I'M GRATEFUL FOR:

- [ ]
- [ ]
- [ ]

EVENING REFLECTION

GOOD THINGS THAT HAPPENED TODAY:

HOW FOCUSING ON GRATITUDE MADE ME FEEL:

A POSITIVE THOUGHT TO CARRY ME TO SLEEP:

30-DAY REFLECTION

MONTH:

REFLECTIONS ON THE EFFECTS GRATITUDE HAS HAD ON MY OVERALL WELL BEING AND THE IMPACT IT HAS HAD ON MY EVERYDAY LIFE.

MORNING MEDITATION

DATE ___/___/___

TODAY'S FOCUS:

WHAT I'M GRATEFUL FOR:

- [ ]
- [ ]
- [ ]

EVENING REFLECTION

GOOD THINGS THAT HAPPENED TODAY:

HOW FOCUSING ON GRATITUDE MADE ME FEEL:

A POSITIVE THOUGHT TO CARRY ME TO SLEEP:

MORNING MEDITATION

DATE ___/___/___

TODAY'S FOCUS:

WHAT I'M GRATEFUL FOR:

- [ ]
- [ ]
- [ ]

EVENING REFLECTION

GOOD THINGS THAT HAPPENED TODAY:

HOW FOCUSING ON GRATITUDE MADE ME FEEL:

A POSITIVE THOUGHT TO CARRY ME TO SLEEP:

MORNING MEDITATION

DATE ___/___/___

TODAY'S FOCUS:

WHAT I'M GRATEFUL FOR:

- [ ]
- [ ]
- [ ]

EVENING REFLECTION

GOOD THINGS THAT HAPPENED TODAY:

HOW FOCUSING ON GRATITUDE MADE ME FEEL:

A POSITIVE THOUGHT TO CARRY ME TO SLEEP:

MORNING MEDITATION

DATE ___/___/___

TODAY'S FOCUS:

WHAT I'M GRATEFUL FOR:

EVENING REFLECTION

GOOD THINGS THAT HAPPENED TODAY:

HOW FOCUSING ON GRATITUDE MADE ME FEEL:

A POSITIVE THOUGHT TO CARRY ME TO SLEEP:

MORNING MEDITATION

DATE ___/___/___

TODAY'S FOCUS:

WHAT I'M GRATEFUL FOR:

- [ ]
- [ ]
- [ ]

EVENING REFLECTION

GOOD THINGS THAT HAPPENED TODAY:

HOW FOCUSING ON GRATITUDE MADE ME FEEL:

A POSITIVE THOUGHT TO CARRY ME TO SLEEP:

MORNING MEDITATION

DATE __/__/__

TODAY'S FOCUS:

WHAT I'M GRATEFUL FOR:

- [ ]
- [ ]
- [ ]

EVENING REFLECTION

GOOD THINGS THAT HAPPENED TODAY:

HOW FOCUSING ON GRATITUDE MADE ME FEEL:

A POSITIVE THOUGHT TO CARRY ME TO SLEEP:

MORNING MEDITATION

DATE ___/___/___

TODAY'S FOCUS:

WHAT I'M GRATEFUL FOR:

- [ ]
- [ ]
- [ ]

EVENING REFLECTION

GOOD THINGS THAT HAPPENED TODAY:

HOW FOCUSING ON GRATITUDE MADE ME FEEL:

A POSITIVE THOUGHT TO CARRY ME TO SLEEP:

MORNING MEDITATION

DATE ___/___/___

TODAY'S FOCUS:

WHAT I'M GRATEFUL FOR:

- [ ]
- [ ]
- [ ]

EVENING REFLECTION

GOOD THINGS THAT HAPPENED TODAY:

HOW FOCUSING ON GRATITUDE MADE ME FEEL:

A POSITIVE THOUGHT TO CARRY ME TO SLEEP:

MORNING MEDITATION

DATE __/__/__

TODAY'S FOCUS:

WHAT I'M GRATEFUL FOR:

- [ ]
- [ ]
- [ ]

EVENING REFLECTION

GOOD THINGS THAT HAPPENED TODAY:

HOW FOCUSING ON GRATITUDE MADE ME FEEL:

A POSITIVE THOUGHT TO CARRY ME TO SLEEP:

MORNING MEDITATION

DATE __/__/__

TODAY'S FOCUS:

WHAT I'M GRATEFUL FOR:

- [ ]
- [ ]
- [ ]

EVENING REFLECTION

GOOD THINGS THAT HAPPENED TODAY:

HOW FOCUSING ON GRATITUDE MADE ME FEEL:

A POSITIVE THOUGHT TO CARRY ME TO SLEEP:

MORNING MEDITATION

DATE ___/___/___

TODAY'S FOCUS:

WHAT I'M GRATEFUL FOR:

- ☐
- ☐
- ☐

EVENING REFLECTION

GOOD THINGS THAT HAPPENED TODAY:

HOW FOCUSING ON GRATITUDE MADE ME FEEL:

A POSITIVE THOUGHT TO CARRY ME TO SLEEP:

MORNING MEDITATION

DATE __/__/__

TODAY'S FOCUS:

WHAT I'M GRATEFUL FOR:

- [ ]
- [ ]
- [ ]

EVENING REFLECTION

GOOD THINGS THAT HAPPENED TODAY:

HOW FOCUSING ON GRATITUDE MADE ME FEEL:

A POSITIVE THOUGHT TO CARRY ME TO SLEEP:

MORNING MEDITATION

DATE ___/___/___

TODAY'S FOCUS:

WHAT I'M GRATEFUL FOR:

- [ ]
- [ ]
- [ ]

EVENING REFLECTION

GOOD THINGS THAT HAPPENED TODAY:

HOW FOCUSING ON GRATITUDE MADE ME FEEL:

A POSITIVE THOUGHT TO CARRY ME TO SLEEP:

MORNING MEDITATION

DATE __/__/__

TODAY'S FOCUS:

WHAT I'M GRATEFUL FOR:

- [ ]
- [ ]
- [ ]

EVENING REFLECTION

GOOD THINGS THAT HAPPENED TODAY:

HOW FOCUSING ON GRATITUDE MADE ME FEEL:

A POSITIVE THOUGHT TO CARRY ME TO SLEEP:

MORNING MEDITATION

DATE __/__/__

TODAY'S FOCUS:

WHAT I'M GRATEFUL FOR:

- [ ]
- [ ]
- [ ]

EVENING REFLECTION

GOOD THINGS THAT HAPPENED TODAY:

HOW FOCUSING ON GRATITUDE MADE ME FEEL:

A POSITIVE THOUGHT TO CARRY ME TO SLEEP:

MORNING MEDITATION

DATE __/__/__

TODAY'S FOCUS:

WHAT I'M GRATEFUL FOR:

- [ ]
- [ ]
- [ ]

EVENING REFLECTION

GOOD THINGS THAT HAPPENED TODAY:

HOW FOCUSING ON GRATITUDE MADE ME FEEL:

A POSITIVE THOUGHT TO CARRY ME TO SLEEP:

MORNING MEDITATION

DATE ___/___/___

TODAY'S FOCUS:

WHAT I'M GRATEFUL FOR:

- [ ]
- [ ]
- [ ]

EVENING REFLECTION

GOOD THINGS THAT HAPPENED TODAY:

HOW FOCUSING ON GRATITUDE MADE ME FEEL:

A POSITIVE THOUGHT TO CARRY ME TO SLEEP:

MORNING MEDITATION

DATE ___/___/___

TODAY'S FOCUS:

WHAT I'M GRATEFUL FOR:

☐

☐

☐

EVENING REFLECTION

GOOD THINGS THAT HAPPENED TODAY:

HOW FOCUSING ON GRATITUDE MADE ME FEEL:

A POSITIVE THOUGHT TO CARRY ME TO SLEEP:

MORNING MEDITATION

DATE ___/___/___

TODAY'S FOCUS:

WHAT I'M GRATEFUL FOR:

- [ ]
- [ ]
- [ ]

EVENING REFLECTION

GOOD THINGS THAT HAPPENED TODAY:

HOW FOCUSING ON GRATITUDE MADE ME FEEL:

A POSITIVE THOUGHT TO CARRY ME TO SLEEP:

MORNING MEDITATION

DATE __/__/__

TODAY'S FOCUS:

WHAT I'M GRATEFUL FOR:

☐

☐

☐

EVENING REFLECTION

GOOD THINGS THAT HAPPENED TODAY:

HOW FOCUSING ON GRATITUDE MADE ME FEEL:

A POSITIVE THOUGHT TO CARRY ME TO SLEEP:

MORNING MEDITATION

DATE ___/___/___

TODAY'S FOCUS:

WHAT I'M GRATEFUL FOR:

- [ ]
- [ ]
- [ ]

EVENING REFLECTION

GOOD THINGS THAT HAPPENED TODAY:

HOW FOCUSING ON GRATITUDE MADE ME FEEL:

A POSITIVE THOUGHT TO CARRY ME TO SLEEP:

MORNING MEDITATION

DATE ___/___/___

TODAY'S FOCUS:

WHAT I'M GRATEFUL FOR:

- [ ]
- [ ]
- [ ]

EVENING REFLECTION

GOOD THINGS THAT HAPPENED TODAY:

HOW FOCUSING ON GRATITUDE MADE ME FEEL:

A POSITIVE THOUGHT TO CARRY ME TO SLEEP:

MORNING MEDITATION

DATE ___/___/___

TODAY'S FOCUS:

WHAT I'M GRATEFUL FOR:

- [ ]
- [ ]
- [ ]

EVENING REFLECTION

GOOD THINGS THAT HAPPENED TODAY:

HOW FOCUSING ON GRATITUDE MADE ME FEEL:

A POSITIVE THOUGHT TO CARRY ME TO SLEEP:

MORNING MEDITATION

DATE __/__/__

TODAY'S FOCUS:

WHAT I'M GRATEFUL FOR:

- [ ]
- [ ]
- [ ]

EVENING REFLECTION

GOOD THINGS THAT HAPPENED TODAY:

HOW FOCUSING ON GRATITUDE MADE ME FEEL:

A POSITIVE THOUGHT TO CARRY ME TO SLEEP:

MORNING MEDITATION

DATE ___/___/___

TODAY'S FOCUS:

WHAT I'M GRATEFUL FOR:

- [ ]
- [ ]
- [ ]

EVENING REFLECTION

GOOD THINGS THAT HAPPENED TODAY:

HOW FOCUSING ON GRATITUDE MADE ME FEEL:

A POSITIVE THOUGHT TO CARRY ME TO SLEEP:

MORNING MEDITATION

DATE __/__/__

TODAY'S FOCUS:

WHAT I'M GRATEFUL FOR:

- [ ]
- [ ]
- [ ]

EVENING REFLECTION

GOOD THINGS THAT HAPPENED TODAY:

HOW FOCUSING ON GRATITUDE MADE ME FEEL:

A POSITIVE THOUGHT TO CARRY ME TO SLEEP:

MORNING MEDITATION

DATE ___/___/___

TODAY'S FOCUS:

WHAT I'M GRATEFUL FOR:

- [ ]
- [ ]
- [ ]

EVENING REFLECTION

GOOD THINGS THAT HAPPENED TODAY:

HOW FOCUSING ON GRATITUDE MADE ME FEEL:

A POSITIVE THOUGHT TO CARRY ME TO SLEEP:

MORNING MEDITATION

DATE __/__/__

TODAY'S FOCUS:

WHAT I'M GRATEFUL FOR:

☐

☐

☐

EVENING REFLECTION

GOOD THINGS THAT HAPPENED TODAY:

HOW FOCUSING ON GRATITUDE MADE ME FEEL:

A POSITIVE THOUGHT TO CARRY ME TO SLEEP:

MORNING MEDITATION

DATE ___/___/___

TODAY'S FOCUS:

WHAT I'M GRATEFUL FOR:

- [ ]
- [ ]
- [ ]

EVENING REFLECTION

GOOD THINGS THAT HAPPENED TODAY:

HOW FOCUSING ON GRATITUDE MADE ME FEEL:

A POSITIVE THOUGHT TO CARRY ME TO SLEEP:

MORNING MEDITATION

DATE ___/___/___

TODAY'S FOCUS:

WHAT I'M GRATEFUL FOR:

EVENING REFLECTION

GOOD THINGS THAT HAPPENED TODAY:

HOW FOCUSING ON GRATITUDE MADE ME FEEL:

A POSITIVE THOUGHT TO CARRY ME TO SLEEP:

30-DAY REFLECTION

MONTH:

REFLECTIONS ON THE EFFECTS GRATITUDE HAS HAD ON MY OVERALL WELL BEING AND THE IMPACT IT HAS HAD ON MY EVERYDAY LIFE.

MORNING MEDITATION

DATE __/__/__

TODAY'S FOCUS:

WHAT I'M GRATEFUL FOR:

- [ ]
- [ ]
- [ ]

EVENING REFLECTION

GOOD THINGS THAT HAPPENED TODAY:

HOW FOCUSING ON GRATITUDE MADE ME FEEL:

A POSITIVE THOUGHT TO CARRY ME TO SLEEP:

MORNING MEDITATION

DATE ___/___/___

TODAY'S FOCUS:

WHAT I'M GRATEFUL FOR:

- [ ]
- [ ]
- [ ]

EVENING REFLECTION

GOOD THINGS THAT HAPPENED TODAY:

HOW FOCUSING ON GRATITUDE MADE ME FEEL:

A POSITIVE THOUGHT TO CARRY ME TO SLEEP:

MORNING MEDITATION

DATE __/__/__

TODAY'S FOCUS:

WHAT I'M GRATEFUL FOR:

- [ ]
- [ ]
- [ ]

EVENING REFLECTION

GOOD THINGS THAT HAPPENED TODAY:

HOW FOCUSING ON GRATITUDE MADE ME FEEL:

A POSITIVE THOUGHT TO CARRY ME TO SLEEP:

MORNING MEDITATION

DATE __/__/__

TODAY'S FOCUS:

WHAT I'M GRATEFUL FOR:

- [ ]
- [ ]
- [ ]

EVENING REFLECTION

GOOD THINGS THAT HAPPENED TODAY:

HOW FOCUSING ON GRATITUDE MADE ME FEEL:

A POSITIVE THOUGHT TO CARRY ME TO SLEEP:

MORNING MEDITATION

DATE ___/___/___

TODAY'S FOCUS:

WHAT I'M GRATEFUL FOR:

- [ ]
- [ ]
- [ ]

EVENING REFLECTION

GOOD THINGS THAT HAPPENED TODAY:

HOW FOCUSING ON GRATITUDE MADE ME FEEL:

A POSITIVE THOUGHT TO CARRY ME TO SLEEP:

MORNING MEDITATION

DATE __/__/__

TODAY'S FOCUS:

WHAT I'M GRATEFUL FOR:

- [ ]
- [ ]
- [ ]

EVENING REFLECTION

GOOD THINGS THAT HAPPENED TODAY:

HOW FOCUSING ON GRATITUDE MADE ME FEEL:

A POSITIVE THOUGHT TO CARRY ME TO SLEEP:

MORNING MEDITATION

DATE ___/___/___

TODAY'S FOCUS:

WHAT I'M GRATEFUL FOR:

- [ ]
- [ ]
- [ ]

EVENING REFLECTION

GOOD THINGS THAT HAPPENED TODAY:

HOW FOCUSING ON GRATITUDE MADE ME FEEL:

A POSITIVE THOUGHT TO CARRY ME TO SLEEP:

MORNING MEDITATION

DATE ___/___/___

TODAY'S FOCUS:

WHAT I'M GRATEFUL FOR:

- [ ]
- [ ]
- [ ]

EVENING REFLECTION

GOOD THINGS THAT HAPPENED TODAY:

HOW FOCUSING ON GRATITUDE MADE ME FEEL:

A POSITIVE THOUGHT TO CARRY ME TO SLEEP:

MORNING MEDITATION

DATE __/__/__

TODAY'S FOCUS:

WHAT I'M GRATEFUL FOR:

- [ ]
- [ ]
- [ ]

EVENING REFLECTION

GOOD THINGS THAT HAPPENED TODAY:

HOW FOCUSING ON GRATITUDE MADE ME FEEL:

A POSITIVE THOUGHT TO CARRY ME TO SLEEP:

MORNING MEDITATION

DATE __/__/__

TODAY'S FOCUS:

WHAT I'M GRATEFUL FOR:

- [ ]
- [ ]
- [ ]

EVENING REFLECTION

GOOD THINGS THAT HAPPENED TODAY:

HOW FOCUSING ON GRATITUDE MADE ME FEEL:

A POSITIVE THOUGHT TO CARRY ME TO SLEEP:

MORNING MEDITATION

DATE __/__/__

TODAY'S FOCUS:

WHAT I'M GRATEFUL FOR:

- [ ]
- [ ]
- [ ]

EVENING REFLECTION

GOOD THINGS THAT HAPPENED TODAY:

HOW FOCUSING ON GRATITUDE MADE ME FEEL:

A POSITIVE THOUGHT TO CARRY ME TO SLEEP:

MORNING MEDITATION

DATE __/__/__

TODAY'S FOCUS:

WHAT I'M GRATEFUL FOR:

- [ ]
- [ ]
- [ ]

EVENING REFLECTION

GOOD THINGS THAT HAPPENED TODAY:

HOW FOCUSING ON GRATITUDE MADE ME FEEL:

A POSITIVE THOUGHT TO CARRY ME TO SLEEP:

MORNING MEDITATION

DATE __/__/__

TODAY'S FOCUS:

WHAT I'M GRATEFUL FOR:

- [ ]
- [ ]
- [ ]

EVENING REFLECTION

GOOD THINGS THAT HAPPENED TODAY:

HOW FOCUSING ON GRATITUDE MADE ME FEEL:

A POSITIVE THOUGHT TO CARRY ME TO SLEEP:

MORNING MEDITATION

DATE ___/___/___

TODAY'S FOCUS:

WHAT I'M GRATEFUL FOR:

- [ ]
- [ ]
- [ ]

EVENING REFLECTION

GOOD THINGS THAT HAPPENED TODAY:

HOW FOCUSING ON GRATITUDE MADE ME FEEL:

A POSITIVE THOUGHT TO CARRY ME TO SLEEP:

MORNING MEDITATION

DATE ___/___/___

TODAY'S FOCUS:

WHAT I'M GRATEFUL FOR:

- [ ]
- [ ]
- [ ]

EVENING REFLECTION

GOOD THINGS THAT HAPPENED TODAY:

HOW FOCUSING ON GRATITUDE MADE ME FEEL:

A POSITIVE THOUGHT TO CARRY ME TO SLEEP:

MORNING MEDITATION

DATE ___/___/___

TODAY'S FOCUS:

WHAT I'M GRATEFUL FOR:

- [ ]
- [ ]
- [ ]

EVENING REFLECTION

GOOD THINGS THAT HAPPENED TODAY:

HOW FOCUSING ON GRATITUDE MADE ME FEEL:

A POSITIVE THOUGHT TO CARRY ME TO SLEEP:

MORNING MEDITATION

DATE ___/___/___

TODAY'S FOCUS:

WHAT I'M GRATEFUL FOR:

- [ ]
- [ ]
- [ ]

EVENING REFLECTION

GOOD THINGS THAT HAPPENED TODAY:

HOW FOCUSING ON GRATITUDE MADE ME FEEL:

A POSITIVE THOUGHT TO CARRY ME TO SLEEP:

MORNING MEDITATION

DATE __/__/__

TODAY'S FOCUS:

WHAT I'M GRATEFUL FOR:

- [ ]
- [ ]
- [ ]

EVENING REFLECTION

GOOD THINGS THAT HAPPENED TODAY:

HOW FOCUSING ON GRATITUDE MADE ME FEEL:

A POSITIVE THOUGHT TO CARRY ME TO SLEEP:

MORNING MEDITATION

DATE ___/___/___

TODAY'S FOCUS:

WHAT I'M GRATEFUL FOR:

- [ ]
- [ ]
- [ ]

EVENING REFLECTION

GOOD THINGS THAT HAPPENED TODAY:

HOW FOCUSING ON GRATITUDE MADE ME FEEL:

A POSITIVE THOUGHT TO CARRY ME TO SLEEP:

MORNING MEDITATION

DATE __/__/__

TODAY'S FOCUS:

WHAT I'M GRATEFUL FOR:

- [ ]
- [ ]
- [ ]

EVENING REFLECTION

GOOD THINGS THAT HAPPENED TODAY:

HOW FOCUSING ON GRATITUDE MADE ME FEEL:

A POSITIVE THOUGHT TO CARRY ME TO SLEEP:

MORNING MEDITATION

DATE ___/___/___

TODAY'S FOCUS:

WHAT I'M GRATEFUL FOR:

- [ ]
- [ ]
- [ ]

EVENING REFLECTION

GOOD THINGS THAT HAPPENED TODAY:

HOW FOCUSING ON GRATITUDE MADE ME FEEL:

A POSITIVE THOUGHT TO CARRY ME TO SLEEP:

MORNING MEDITATION

DATE __/__/__

TODAY'S FOCUS:

WHAT I'M GRATEFUL FOR:

- [ ]
- [ ]
- [ ]

EVENING REFLECTION

GOOD THINGS THAT HAPPENED TODAY:

HOW FOCUSING ON GRATITUDE MADE ME FEEL:

A POSITIVE THOUGHT TO CARRY ME TO SLEEP:

MORNING MEDITATION

DATE ___/___/___

TODAY'S FOCUS:

WHAT I'M GRATEFUL FOR:

- [ ]
- [ ]
- [ ]

EVENING REFLECTION

GOOD THINGS THAT HAPPENED TODAY:

HOW FOCUSING ON GRATITUDE MADE ME FEEL:

A POSITIVE THOUGHT TO CARRY ME TO SLEEP:

MORNING MEDITATION

DATE ___/___/___

TODAY'S FOCUS:

WHAT I'M GRATEFUL FOR:

- [ ]
- [ ]
- [ ]

EVENING REFLECTION

GOOD THINGS THAT HAPPENED TODAY:

HOW FOCUSING ON GRATITUDE MADE ME FEEL:

A POSITIVE THOUGHT TO CARRY ME TO SLEEP:

MORNING MEDITATION

DATE __/__/__

TODAY'S FOCUS:

WHAT I'M GRATEFUL FOR:

- [ ]
- [ ]
- [ ]

EVENING REFLECTION

GOOD THINGS THAT HAPPENED TODAY:

HOW FOCUSING ON GRATITUDE MADE ME FEEL:

A POSITIVE THOUGHT TO CARRY ME TO SLEEP:

MORNING MEDITATION

DATE ___/___/___

TODAY'S FOCUS:

WHAT I'M GRATEFUL FOR:

- [ ]
- [ ]
- [ ]

EVENING REFLECTION

GOOD THINGS THAT HAPPENED TODAY:

HOW FOCUSING ON GRATITUDE MADE ME FEEL:

A POSITIVE THOUGHT TO CARRY ME TO SLEEP:

MORNING MEDITATION

DATE __/__/__

TODAY'S FOCUS:

WHAT I'M GRATEFUL FOR:

- ☐
- ☐
- ☐

EVENING REFLECTION

GOOD THINGS THAT HAPPENED TODAY:

HOW FOCUSING ON GRATITUDE MADE ME FEEL:

A POSITIVE THOUGHT TO CARRY ME TO SLEEP:

MORNING MEDITATION

DATE ___/___/___

TODAY'S FOCUS:

WHAT I'M GRATEFUL FOR:

☐

☐

☐

EVENING REFLECTION

GOOD THINGS THAT HAPPENED TODAY:

HOW FOCUSING ON GRATITUDE MADE ME FEEL:

A POSITIVE THOUGHT TO CARRY ME TO SLEEP:

MORNING MEDITATION

DATE ___/___/___

TODAY'S FOCUS:

WHAT I'M GRATEFUL FOR:

- [ ]
- [ ]
- [ ]

EVENING REFLECTION

GOOD THINGS THAT HAPPENED TODAY:

HOW FOCUSING ON GRATITUDE MADE ME FEEL:

A POSITIVE THOUGHT TO CARRY ME TO SLEEP:

MORNING MEDITATION

DATE ___/___/___

TODAY'S FOCUS:

WHAT I'M GRATEFUL FOR:

- [ ]
- [ ]
- [ ]

EVENING REFLECTION

GOOD THINGS THAT HAPPENED TODAY:

HOW FOCUSING ON GRATITUDE MADE ME FEEL:

A POSITIVE THOUGHT TO CARRY ME TO SLEEP:

30-DAY REFLECTION

MONTH:

REFLECTIONS ON THE EFFECTS GRATITUDE HAS HAD ON MY OVERALL WELL BEING AND THE IMPACT IT HAS HAD ON MY EVERYDAY LIFE.

MORNING MEDITATION

DATE ___/___/___

TODAY'S FOCUS:

WHAT I'M GRATEFUL FOR:

- [ ]
- [ ]
- [ ]

EVENING REFLECTION

GOOD THINGS THAT HAPPENED TODAY:

HOW FOCUSING ON GRATITUDE MADE ME FEEL:

A POSITIVE THOUGHT TO CARRY ME TO SLEEP:

MORNING MEDITATION

DATE __/__/__

TODAY'S FOCUS:

WHAT I'M GRATEFUL FOR:

EVENING REFLECTION

GOOD THINGS THAT HAPPENED TODAY:

HOW FOCUSING ON GRATITUDE MADE ME FEEL:

A POSITIVE THOUGHT TO CARRY ME TO SLEEP:

MORNING MEDITATION

DATE __/__/__

TODAY'S FOCUS:

WHAT I'M GRATEFUL FOR:

- [ ]
- [ ]
- [ ]

EVENING REFLECTION

GOOD THINGS THAT HAPPENED TODAY:

HOW FOCUSING ON GRATITUDE MADE ME FEEL:

A POSITIVE THOUGHT TO CARRY ME TO SLEEP:

MORNING MEDITATION

DATE __/__/__

TODAY'S FOCUS:

WHAT I'M GRATEFUL FOR:

EVENING REFLECTION

GOOD THINGS THAT HAPPENED TODAY:

HOW FOCUSING ON GRATITUDE MADE ME FEEL:

A POSITIVE THOUGHT TO CARRY ME TO SLEEP:

MORNING MEDITATION

DATE ___/___/___

TODAY'S FOCUS:

WHAT I'M GRATEFUL FOR:

- [ ]
- [ ]
- [ ]

EVENING REFLECTION

GOOD THINGS THAT HAPPENED TODAY:

HOW FOCUSING ON GRATITUDE MADE ME FEEL:

A POSITIVE THOUGHT TO CARRY ME TO SLEEP:

MORNING MEDITATION

DATE __/__/__

TODAY'S FOCUS:

WHAT I'M GRATEFUL FOR:

☐

☐

☐

EVENING REFLECTION

GOOD THINGS THAT HAPPENED TODAY:

HOW FOCUSING ON GRATITUDE MADE ME FEEL:

A POSITIVE THOUGHT TO CARRY ME TO SLEEP:

MORNING MEDITATION

DATE ___/___/___

TODAY'S FOCUS:

WHAT I'M GRATEFUL FOR:

- [ ]
- [ ]
- [ ]

EVENING REFLECTION

GOOD THINGS THAT HAPPENED TODAY:

HOW FOCUSING ON GRATITUDE MADE ME FEEL:

A POSITIVE THOUGHT TO CARRY ME TO SLEEP:

MORNING MEDITATION

DATE ___/___/___

TODAY'S FOCUS:

WHAT I'M GRATEFUL FOR:

- [ ]
- [ ]
- [ ]

EVENING REFLECTION

GOOD THINGS THAT HAPPENED TODAY:

HOW FOCUSING ON GRATITUDE MADE ME FEEL:

A POSITIVE THOUGHT TO CARRY ME TO SLEEP:

MORNING MEDITATION

DATE ___/___/___

TODAY'S FOCUS:

WHAT I'M GRATEFUL FOR:

- [ ]
- [ ]
- [ ]

EVENING REFLECTION

GOOD THINGS THAT HAPPENED TODAY:

HOW FOCUSING ON GRATITUDE MADE ME FEEL:

A POSITIVE THOUGHT TO CARRY ME TO SLEEP:

MORNING MEDITATION

DATE ___/___/___

TODAY'S FOCUS:

WHAT I'M GRATEFUL FOR:

- [ ]
- [ ]
- [ ]

EVENING REFLECTION

GOOD THINGS THAT HAPPENED TODAY:

HOW FOCUSING ON GRATITUDE MADE ME FEEL:

A POSITIVE THOUGHT TO CARRY ME TO SLEEP:

MORNING MEDITATION

DATE ___/___/___

TODAY'S FOCUS:

WHAT I'M GRATEFUL FOR:

- [ ]
- [ ]
- [ ]

EVENING REFLECTION

GOOD THINGS THAT HAPPENED TODAY:

HOW FOCUSING ON GRATITUDE MADE ME FEEL:

A POSITIVE THOUGHT TO CARRY ME TO SLEEP:

MORNING MEDITATION

DATE __/__/__

TODAY'S FOCUS:

WHAT I'M GRATEFUL FOR:

- [ ]
- [ ]
- [ ]

EVENING REFLECTION

GOOD THINGS THAT HAPPENED TODAY:

HOW FOCUSING ON GRATITUDE MADE ME FEEL:

A POSITIVE THOUGHT TO CARRY ME TO SLEEP:

MORNING MEDITATION

DATE __/__/__

TODAY'S FOCUS:

WHAT I'M GRATEFUL FOR:

- [ ]
- [ ]
- [ ]

EVENING REFLECTION

GOOD THINGS THAT HAPPENED TODAY:

HOW FOCUSING ON GRATITUDE MADE ME FEEL:

A POSITIVE THOUGHT TO CARRY ME TO SLEEP:

MORNING MEDITATION

DATE ___/___/___

TODAY'S FOCUS:

WHAT I'M GRATEFUL FOR:

- [ ]
- [ ]
- [ ]

EVENING REFLECTION

GOOD THINGS THAT HAPPENED TODAY:

HOW FOCUSING ON GRATITUDE MADE ME FEEL:

A POSITIVE THOUGHT TO CARRY ME TO SLEEP:

MORNING MEDITATION

DATE ___/___/___

TODAY'S FOCUS:

WHAT I'M GRATEFUL FOR:

- [ ]
- [ ]
- [ ]

EVENING REFLECTION

GOOD THINGS THAT HAPPENED TODAY:

HOW FOCUSING ON GRATITUDE MADE ME FEEL:

A POSITIVE THOUGHT TO CARRY ME TO SLEEP:

MORNING MEDITATION

DATE ___/___/___

TODAY'S FOCUS:

WHAT I'M GRATEFUL FOR:

- [ ]
- [ ]
- [ ]

EVENING REFLECTION

GOOD THINGS THAT HAPPENED TODAY:

HOW FOCUSING ON GRATITUDE MADE ME FEEL:

A POSITIVE THOUGHT TO CARRY ME TO SLEEP:

MORNING MEDITATION

DATE __/__/__

TODAY'S FOCUS:

WHAT I'M GRATEFUL FOR:

- [ ]
- [ ]
- [ ]

EVENING REFLECTION

GOOD THINGS THAT HAPPENED TODAY:

HOW FOCUSING ON GRATITUDE MADE ME FEEL:

A POSITIVE THOUGHT TO CARRY ME TO SLEEP:

MORNING MEDITATION

DATE __/__/__

TODAY'S FOCUS:

WHAT I'M GRATEFUL FOR:

- [ ]
- [ ]
- [ ]

EVENING REFLECTION

GOOD THINGS THAT HAPPENED TODAY:

HOW FOCUSING ON GRATITUDE MADE ME FEEL:

A POSITIVE THOUGHT TO CARRY ME TO SLEEP:

MORNING MEDITATION

DATE ___/___/___

TODAY'S FOCUS:

WHAT I'M GRATEFUL FOR:

- [ ]
- [ ]
- [ ]

EVENING REFLECTION

GOOD THINGS THAT HAPPENED TODAY:

HOW FOCUSING ON GRATITUDE MADE ME FEEL:

A POSITIVE THOUGHT TO CARRY ME TO SLEEP:

MORNING MEDITATION

DATE ___/___/___

TODAY'S FOCUS:

WHAT I'M GRATEFUL FOR:

- [ ]
- [ ]
- [ ]

EVENING REFLECTION

GOOD THINGS THAT HAPPENED TODAY:

HOW FOCUSING ON GRATITUDE MADE ME FEEL:

A POSITIVE THOUGHT TO CARRY ME TO SLEEP:

MORNING MEDITATION

DATE ___/___/___

TODAY'S FOCUS:

WHAT I'M GRATEFUL FOR:

- [ ]
- [ ]
- [ ]

EVENING REFLECTION

GOOD THINGS THAT HAPPENED TODAY:

HOW FOCUSING ON GRATITUDE MADE ME FEEL:

A POSITIVE THOUGHT TO CARRY ME TO SLEEP:

MORNING MEDITATION

DATE __/__/__

TODAY'S FOCUS:

WHAT I'M GRATEFUL FOR:

- [ ]
- [ ]
- [ ]

EVENING REFLECTION

GOOD THINGS THAT HAPPENED TODAY:

HOW FOCUSING ON GRATITUDE MADE ME FEEL:

A POSITIVE THOUGHT TO CARRY ME TO SLEEP:

MORNING MEDITATION

DATE ___/___/___

TODAY'S FOCUS:

WHAT I'M GRATEFUL FOR:

- [ ]
- [ ]
- [ ]

EVENING REFLECTION

GOOD THINGS THAT HAPPENED TODAY:

HOW FOCUSING ON GRATITUDE MADE ME FEEL:

A POSITIVE THOUGHT TO CARRY ME TO SLEEP:

MORNING MEDITATION

DATE __/__/__

TODAY'S FOCUS:

WHAT I'M GRATEFUL FOR:

- [ ]
- [ ]
- [ ]

EVENING REFLECTION

GOOD THINGS THAT HAPPENED TODAY:

HOW FOCUSING ON GRATITUDE MADE ME FEEL:

A POSITIVE THOUGHT TO CARRY ME TO SLEEP:

MORNING MEDITATION

DATE ___/___/___

TODAY'S FOCUS:

WHAT I'M GRATEFUL FOR:

- [ ]
- [ ]
- [ ]

EVENING REFLECTION

GOOD THINGS THAT HAPPENED TODAY:

HOW FOCUSING ON GRATITUDE MADE ME FEEL:

A POSITIVE THOUGHT TO CARRY ME TO SLEEP:

MORNING MEDITATION

DATE __/__/__

TODAY'S FOCUS:

WHAT I'M GRATEFUL FOR:

- [ ]
- [ ]
- [ ]

EVENING REFLECTION

GOOD THINGS THAT HAPPENED TODAY:

HOW FOCUSING ON GRATITUDE MADE ME FEEL:

A POSITIVE THOUGHT TO CARRY ME TO SLEEP:

MORNING MEDITATION

DATE ___/___/___

TODAY'S FOCUS:

WHAT I'M GRATEFUL FOR:

☐

☐

☐

EVENING REFLECTION

GOOD THINGS THAT HAPPENED TODAY:

HOW FOCUSING ON GRATITUDE MADE ME FEEL:

A POSITIVE THOUGHT TO CARRY ME TO SLEEP:

MORNING MEDITATION

DATE ___/___/___

TODAY'S FOCUS:

WHAT I'M GRATEFUL FOR:

- [ ]
- [ ]
- [ ]

EVENING REFLECTION

GOOD THINGS THAT HAPPENED TODAY:

HOW FOCUSING ON GRATITUDE MADE ME FEEL:

A POSITIVE THOUGHT TO CARRY ME TO SLEEP:

MORNING MEDITATION

DATE ___/___/___

TODAY'S FOCUS:

WHAT I'M GRATEFUL FOR:

- [ ]
- [ ]
- [ ]

EVENING REFLECTION

GOOD THINGS THAT HAPPENED TODAY:

HOW FOCUSING ON GRATITUDE MADE ME FEEL:

A POSITIVE THOUGHT TO CARRY ME TO SLEEP:

MORNING MEDITATION

DATE __/__/__

TODAY'S FOCUS:

WHAT I'M GRATEFUL FOR:

- [ ]
- [ ]
- [ ]

EVENING REFLECTION

GOOD THINGS THAT HAPPENED TODAY:

HOW FOCUSING ON GRATITUDE MADE ME FEEL:

A POSITIVE THOUGHT TO CARRY ME TO SLEEP:

30-DAY REFLECTION

MONTH:

REFLECTIONS ON THE EFFECTS GRATITUDE HAS HAD ON MY OVERALL WELL BEING AND THE IMPACT IT HAS HAD ON MY EVERYDAY LIFE.

MORNING MEDITATION

DATE __/__/__

TODAY'S FOCUS:

WHAT I'M GRATEFUL FOR:

- [ ]
- [ ]
- [ ]

EVENING REFLECTION

GOOD THINGS THAT HAPPENED TODAY:

HOW FOCUSING ON GRATITUDE MADE ME FEEL:

A POSITIVE THOUGHT TO CARRY ME TO SLEEP:

MORNING MEDITATION

DATE __/__/__

TODAY'S FOCUS:

WHAT I'M GRATEFUL FOR:

☐

☐

☐

EVENING REFLECTION

GOOD THINGS THAT HAPPENED TODAY:

HOW FOCUSING ON GRATITUDE MADE ME FEEL:

A POSITIVE THOUGHT TO CARRY ME TO SLEEP:

MORNING MEDITATION

DATE ___/___/___

TODAY'S FOCUS:

WHAT I'M GRATEFUL FOR:

- [ ]
- [ ]
- [ ]

EVENING REFLECTION

GOOD THINGS THAT HAPPENED TODAY:

HOW FOCUSING ON GRATITUDE MADE ME FEEL:

A POSITIVE THOUGHT TO CARRY ME TO SLEEP:

MORNING MEDITATION

DATE ___/___/___

TODAY'S FOCUS:

WHAT I'M GRATEFUL FOR:

- [ ]
- [ ]
- [ ]

EVENING REFLECTION

GOOD THINGS THAT HAPPENED TODAY:

HOW FOCUSING ON GRATITUDE MADE ME FEEL:

A POSITIVE THOUGHT TO CARRY ME TO SLEEP:

MORNING MEDITATION

DATE ___/___/___

TODAY'S FOCUS:

WHAT I'M GRATEFUL FOR:

- [ ]
- [ ]
- [ ]

EVENING REFLECTION

GOOD THINGS THAT HAPPENED TODAY:

HOW FOCUSING ON GRATITUDE MADE ME FEEL:

A POSITIVE THOUGHT TO CARRY ME TO SLEEP:

MORNING MEDITATION

DATE __/__/__

TODAY'S FOCUS:

WHAT I'M GRATEFUL FOR:

- [ ]
- [ ]
- [ ]

EVENING REFLECTION

GOOD THINGS THAT HAPPENED TODAY:

HOW FOCUSING ON GRATITUDE MADE ME FEEL:

A POSITIVE THOUGHT TO CARRY ME TO SLEEP:

MORNING MEDITATION

DATE ___/___/___

TODAY'S FOCUS:

WHAT I'M GRATEFUL FOR:

- [ ]
- [ ]
- [ ]

EVENING REFLECTION

GOOD THINGS THAT HAPPENED TODAY:

HOW FOCUSING ON GRATITUDE MADE ME FEEL:

A POSITIVE THOUGHT TO CARRY ME TO SLEEP:

MORNING MEDITATION

DATE __/__/__

TODAY'S FOCUS:

WHAT I'M GRATEFUL FOR:

- [ ]
- [ ]
- [ ]

EVENING REFLECTION

GOOD THINGS THAT HAPPENED TODAY:

HOW FOCUSING ON GRATITUDE MADE ME FEEL:

A POSITIVE THOUGHT TO CARRY ME TO SLEEP:

MORNING MEDITATION

DATE __/__/__

TODAY'S FOCUS:

WHAT I'M GRATEFUL FOR:

- [ ]
- [ ]
- [ ]

EVENING REFLECTION

GOOD THINGS THAT HAPPENED TODAY:

HOW FOCUSING ON GRATITUDE MADE ME FEEL:

A POSITIVE THOUGHT TO CARRY ME TO SLEEP:

MORNING MEDITATION

DATE ___/___/___

TODAY'S FOCUS:

WHAT I'M GRATEFUL FOR:

- [ ]
- [ ]
- [ ]

EVENING REFLECTION

GOOD THINGS THAT HAPPENED TODAY:

HOW FOCUSING ON GRATITUDE MADE ME FEEL:

A POSITIVE THOUGHT TO CARRY ME TO SLEEP:

MORNING MEDITATION

DATE ___/___/___

TODAY'S FOCUS:

WHAT I'M GRATEFUL FOR:

- [ ]
- [ ]
- [ ]

EVENING REFLECTION

GOOD THINGS THAT HAPPENED TODAY:

HOW FOCUSING ON GRATITUDE MADE ME FEEL:

A POSITIVE THOUGHT TO CARRY ME TO SLEEP:

MORNING MEDITATION

DATE ___/___/___

TODAY'S FOCUS:

WHAT I'M GRATEFUL FOR:

- [ ]
- [ ]
- [ ]

EVENING REFLECTION

GOOD THINGS THAT HAPPENED TODAY:

HOW FOCUSING ON GRATITUDE MADE ME FEEL:

A POSITIVE THOUGHT TO CARRY ME TO SLEEP:

MORNING MEDITATION

DATE __/__/__

TODAY'S FOCUS:

WHAT I'M GRATEFUL FOR:

- [ ]
- [ ]
- [ ]

EVENING REFLECTION

GOOD THINGS THAT HAPPENED TODAY:

HOW FOCUSING ON GRATITUDE MADE ME FEEL:

A POSITIVE THOUGHT TO CARRY ME TO SLEEP:

MORNING MEDITATION

DATE __/__/__

TODAY'S FOCUS:

WHAT I'M GRATEFUL FOR:

- [ ]
- [ ]
- [ ]

EVENING REFLECTION

GOOD THINGS THAT HAPPENED TODAY:

HOW FOCUSING ON GRATITUDE MADE ME FEEL:

A POSITIVE THOUGHT TO CARRY ME TO SLEEP:

MORNING MEDITATION

DATE __/__/__

TODAY'S FOCUS:

WHAT I'M GRATEFUL FOR:

- [ ]
- [ ]
- [ ]

EVENING REFLECTION

GOOD THINGS THAT HAPPENED TODAY:

HOW FOCUSING ON GRATITUDE MADE ME FEEL:

A POSITIVE THOUGHT TO CARRY ME TO SLEEP:

MORNING MEDITATION

DATE __/__/__

TODAY'S FOCUS:

WHAT I'M GRATEFUL FOR:

- [ ]
- [ ]
- [ ]

EVENING REFLECTION

GOOD THINGS THAT HAPPENED TODAY:

HOW FOCUSING ON GRATITUDE MADE ME FEEL:

A POSITIVE THOUGHT TO CARRY ME TO SLEEP:

MORNING MEDITATION

DATE ___/___/___

TODAY'S FOCUS:

WHAT I'M GRATEFUL FOR:

- [ ]
- [ ]
- [ ]

EVENING REFLECTION

GOOD THINGS THAT HAPPENED TODAY:

HOW FOCUSING ON GRATITUDE MADE ME FEEL:

A POSITIVE THOUGHT TO CARRY ME TO SLEEP:

MORNING MEDITATION

DATE __/__/__

TODAY'S FOCUS:

WHAT I'M GRATEFUL FOR:

- [ ]
- [ ]
- [ ]

EVENING REFLECTION

GOOD THINGS THAT HAPPENED TODAY:

HOW FOCUSING ON GRATITUDE MADE ME FEEL:

A POSITIVE THOUGHT TO CARRY ME TO SLEEP:

MORNING MEDITATION

DATE ___/___/___

TODAY'S FOCUS:

WHAT I'M GRATEFUL FOR:

- [ ]
- [ ]
- [ ]

EVENING REFLECTION

GOOD THINGS THAT HAPPENED TODAY:

HOW FOCUSING ON GRATITUDE MADE ME FEEL:

A POSITIVE THOUGHT TO CARRY ME TO SLEEP:

MORNING MEDITATION

DATE ___/___/___

TODAY'S FOCUS:

WHAT I'M GRATEFUL FOR:

- [ ]
- [ ]
- [ ]

EVENING REFLECTION

GOOD THINGS THAT HAPPENED TODAY:

HOW FOCUSING ON GRATITUDE MADE ME FEEL:

A POSITIVE THOUGHT TO CARRY ME TO SLEEP:

MORNING MEDITATION

DATE __/__/__

TODAY'S FOCUS:

WHAT I'M GRATEFUL FOR:

EVENING REFLECTION

GOOD THINGS THAT HAPPENED TODAY:

HOW FOCUSING ON GRATITUDE MADE ME FEEL:

A POSITIVE THOUGHT TO CARRY ME TO SLEEP:

MORNING MEDITATION

DATE ___/___/___

TODAY'S FOCUS:

WHAT I'M GRATEFUL FOR:

- [ ]
- [ ]
- [ ]

EVENING REFLECTION

GOOD THINGS THAT HAPPENED TODAY:

HOW FOCUSING ON GRATITUDE MADE ME FEEL:

A POSITIVE THOUGHT TO CARRY ME TO SLEEP:

MORNING MEDITATION

DATE __/__/__

TODAY'S FOCUS:

WHAT I'M GRATEFUL FOR:

- [ ]
- [ ]
- [ ]

EVENING REFLECTION

GOOD THINGS THAT HAPPENED TODAY:

HOW FOCUSING ON GRATITUDE MADE ME FEEL:

A POSITIVE THOUGHT TO CARRY ME TO SLEEP:

MORNING MEDITATION

DATE ___/___/___

TODAY'S FOCUS:

WHAT I'M GRATEFUL FOR:

- [ ]
- [ ]
- [ ]

EVENING REFLECTION

GOOD THINGS THAT HAPPENED TODAY:

HOW FOCUSING ON GRATITUDE MADE ME FEEL:

A POSITIVE THOUGHT TO CARRY ME TO SLEEP:

MORNING MEDITATION

DATE __/__/__

TODAY'S FOCUS:

WHAT I'M GRATEFUL FOR:

- [ ]
- [ ]
- [ ]

EVENING REFLECTION

GOOD THINGS THAT HAPPENED TODAY:

HOW FOCUSING ON GRATITUDE MADE ME FEEL:

A POSITIVE THOUGHT TO CARRY ME TO SLEEP:

MORNING MEDITATION

DATE __/__/__

TODAY'S FOCUS:

WHAT I'M GRATEFUL FOR:

- [ ]
- [ ]
- [ ]

EVENING REFLECTION

GOOD THINGS THAT HAPPENED TODAY:

HOW FOCUSING ON GRATITUDE MADE ME FEEL:

A POSITIVE THOUGHT TO CARRY ME TO SLEEP:

MORNING MEDITATION

DATE ___/___/___

TODAY'S FOCUS:

WHAT I'M GRATEFUL FOR:

- [ ]
- [ ]
- [ ]

EVENING REFLECTION

GOOD THINGS THAT HAPPENED TODAY:

HOW FOCUSING ON GRATITUDE MADE ME FEEL:

A POSITIVE THOUGHT TO CARRY ME TO SLEEP:

MORNING MEDITATION

DATE __/__/__

TODAY'S FOCUS:

WHAT I'M GRATEFUL FOR:

- [ ]
- [ ]
- [ ]

EVENING REFLECTION

GOOD THINGS THAT HAPPENED TODAY:

HOW FOCUSING ON GRATITUDE MADE ME FEEL:

A POSITIVE THOUGHT TO CARRY ME TO SLEEP:

MORNING MEDITATION

DATE ___/___/___

TODAY'S FOCUS:

WHAT I'M GRATEFUL FOR:

- [ ]
- [ ]
- [ ]

EVENING REFLECTION

GOOD THINGS THAT HAPPENED TODAY:

HOW FOCUSING ON GRATITUDE MADE ME FEEL:

A POSITIVE THOUGHT TO CARRY ME TO SLEEP:

MORNING MEDITATION

DATE ___/___/___

TODAY'S FOCUS:

WHAT I'M GRATEFUL FOR:

- [ ]
- [ ]
- [ ]

EVENING REFLECTION

GOOD THINGS THAT HAPPENED TODAY:

HOW FOCUSING ON GRATITUDE MADE ME FEEL:

A POSITIVE THOUGHT TO CARRY ME TO SLEEP:

30-DAY REFLECTION

MONTH:

REFLECTIONS ON THE EFFECTS GRATITUDE HAS HAD ON MY OVERALL WELL BEING AND THE IMPACT IT HAS HAD ON MY EVERYDAY LIFE.

MORNING MEDITATION

DATE ___/___/___

TODAY'S FOCUS:

WHAT I'M GRATEFUL FOR:

- [ ]
- [ ]
- [ ]

EVENING REFLECTION

GOOD THINGS THAT HAPPENED TODAY:

HOW FOCUSING ON GRATITUDE MADE ME FEEL:

A POSITIVE THOUGHT TO CARRY ME TO SLEEP:

MORNING MEDITATION

DATE __/__/__

TODAY'S FOCUS:

WHAT I'M GRATEFUL FOR:

- [ ]
- [ ]
- [ ]

EVENING REFLECTION

GOOD THINGS THAT HAPPENED TODAY:

HOW FOCUSING ON GRATITUDE MADE ME FEEL:

A POSITIVE THOUGHT TO CARRY ME TO SLEEP:

MORNING MEDITATION

DATE __/__/__

TODAY'S FOCUS:

WHAT I'M GRATEFUL FOR:

- [ ]
- [ ]
- [ ]

EVENING REFLECTION

GOOD THINGS THAT HAPPENED TODAY:

HOW FOCUSING ON GRATITUDE MADE ME FEEL:

A POSITIVE THOUGHT TO CARRY ME TO SLEEP:

MORNING MEDITATION

DATE __/__/__

TODAY'S FOCUS:

WHAT I'M GRATEFUL FOR:

- [ ]
- [ ]
- [ ]

EVENING REFLECTION

GOOD THINGS THAT HAPPENED TODAY:

HOW FOCUSING ON GRATITUDE MADE ME FEEL:

A POSITIVE THOUGHT TO CARRY ME TO SLEEP:

MORNING MEDITATION

DATE ___/___/___

TODAY'S FOCUS:

WHAT I'M GRATEFUL FOR:

- [ ]
- [ ]
- [ ]

EVENING REFLECTION

GOOD THINGS THAT HAPPENED TODAY:

HOW FOCUSING ON GRATITUDE MADE ME FEEL:

A POSITIVE THOUGHT TO CARRY ME TO SLEEP:

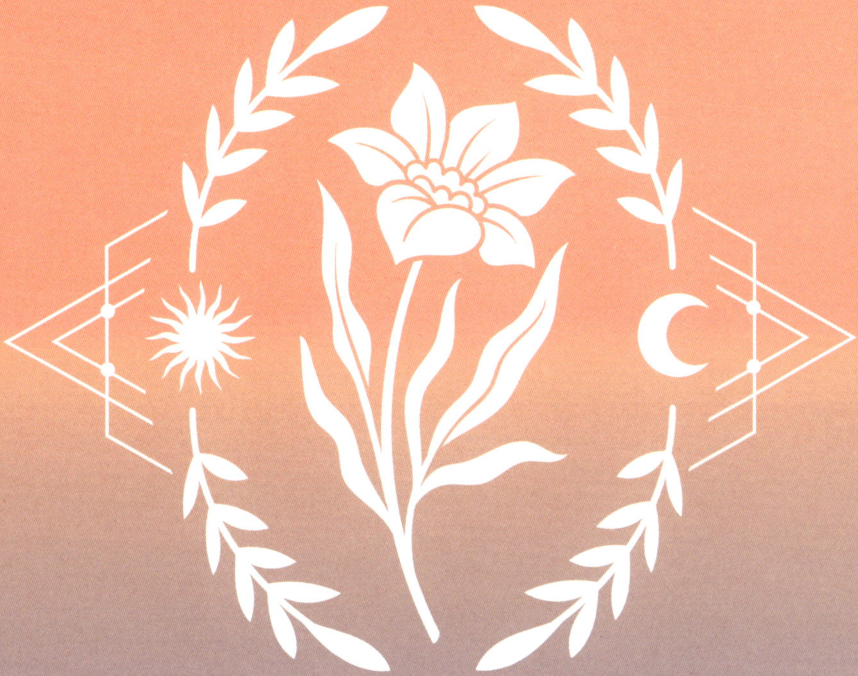

INSIGHTS

A Mandala Journal

www.mandalaearth.com

Art direction and cover design by Ashley Quackenbush
Production design by Amy Tang

MANUFACTURED IN CHINA

10 9 8 7 6 5 4 3 2 1